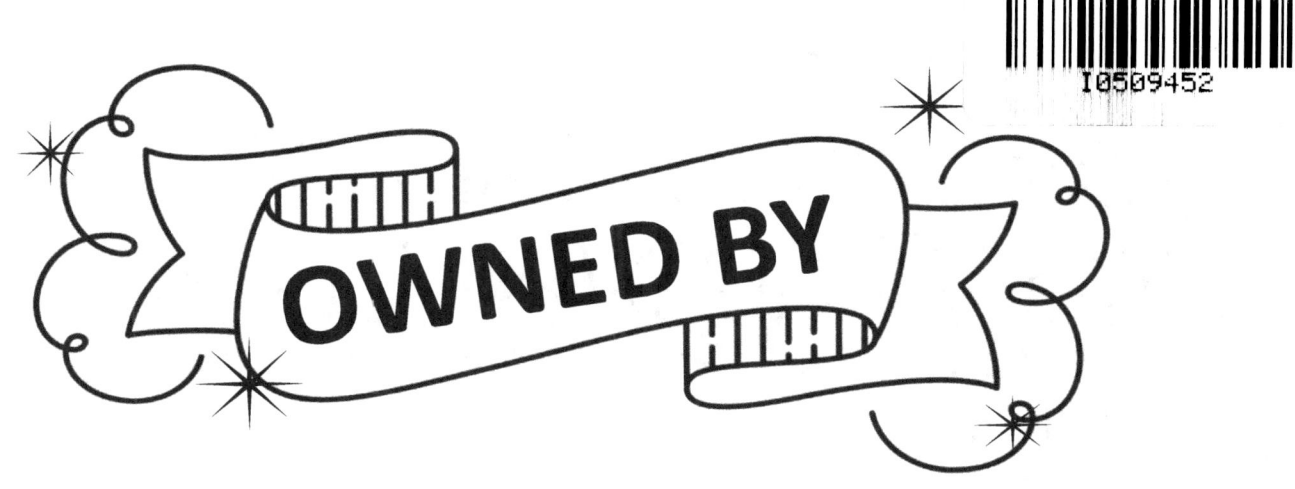

_____

_____

_____
Date

TABLE OF CONTENTS

INTRODUCTION
Activity Book for Young Kids 1

Maze Puzzle 2-25

Spot the Differences 26-45

Sudoku Puzzle 46-66

Cat Shaped Word Search 67-72

Maze Puzzle Solution 73-80

Sudoku Puzzle Solution 81-90

Cat Shaped Word Search Solution 91-95

ACTIVITY BOOK FOR YOUNG KIDS

Spot the Differences, Maze, Sudoku and Word Search Puzzle fun activities for children ages 4-8. Great brain teasers to improve young children motor skills, critical thinking, imagination, logic and number identification.

Packed with hours of fun and creativity in various fun puzzle activities to keep kids engaged and entertained.

Every challenge is more than just a fun game but its a skill set that help young boys and girls to learn while they play.

Have FUN Learning WHiLe yOU pLay

MAZE PUZZLE

Mazes are fun, problem solving games that challenge children to think logical and critical as they try to find their way through the various jumbled chaos. Young children engaging in these games will develop their fine motor and problem solving skills, hand-eye coordination needed for handwriting and printing, as well as improve their concentration as they learn to manipulate their fingers.

The two degrees of difficulty presented on these sheets are the **beginner and easy** level, which makes it more manageable for the age group 4-8 years.

INSTRUCTIONS FOR PLAYING MAZE

Each puzzle contains given instruction in various places. The object is to complete the maze obstacle by finding a path on the graph from the start to the end.

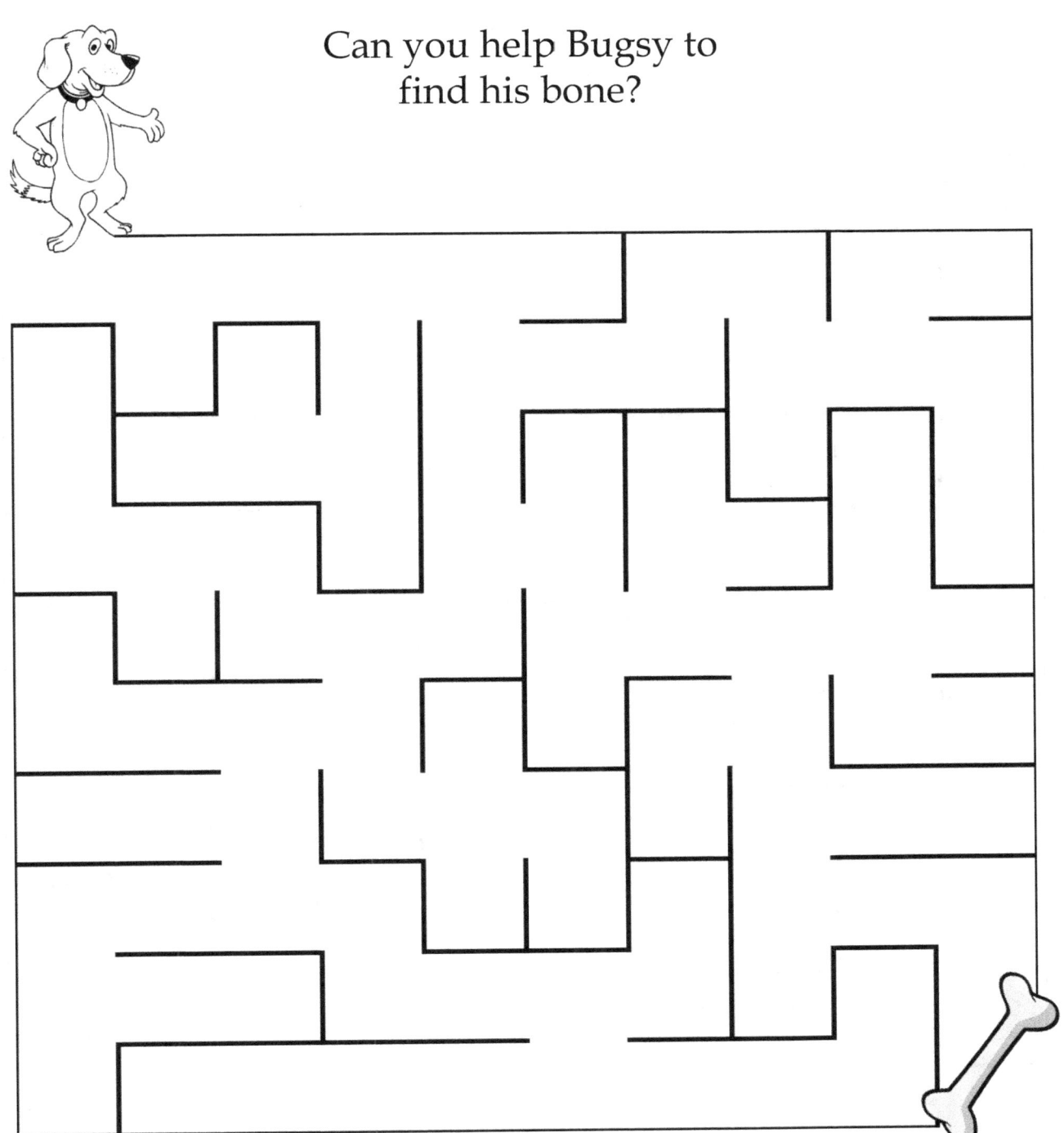

Can you help Bugsy to find his bone?

Puzzle 1 - Beginner

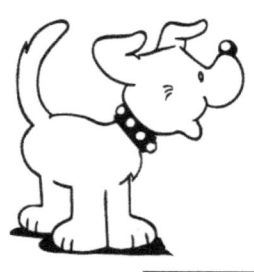

Please feed Puppy Ash. He is hungry.

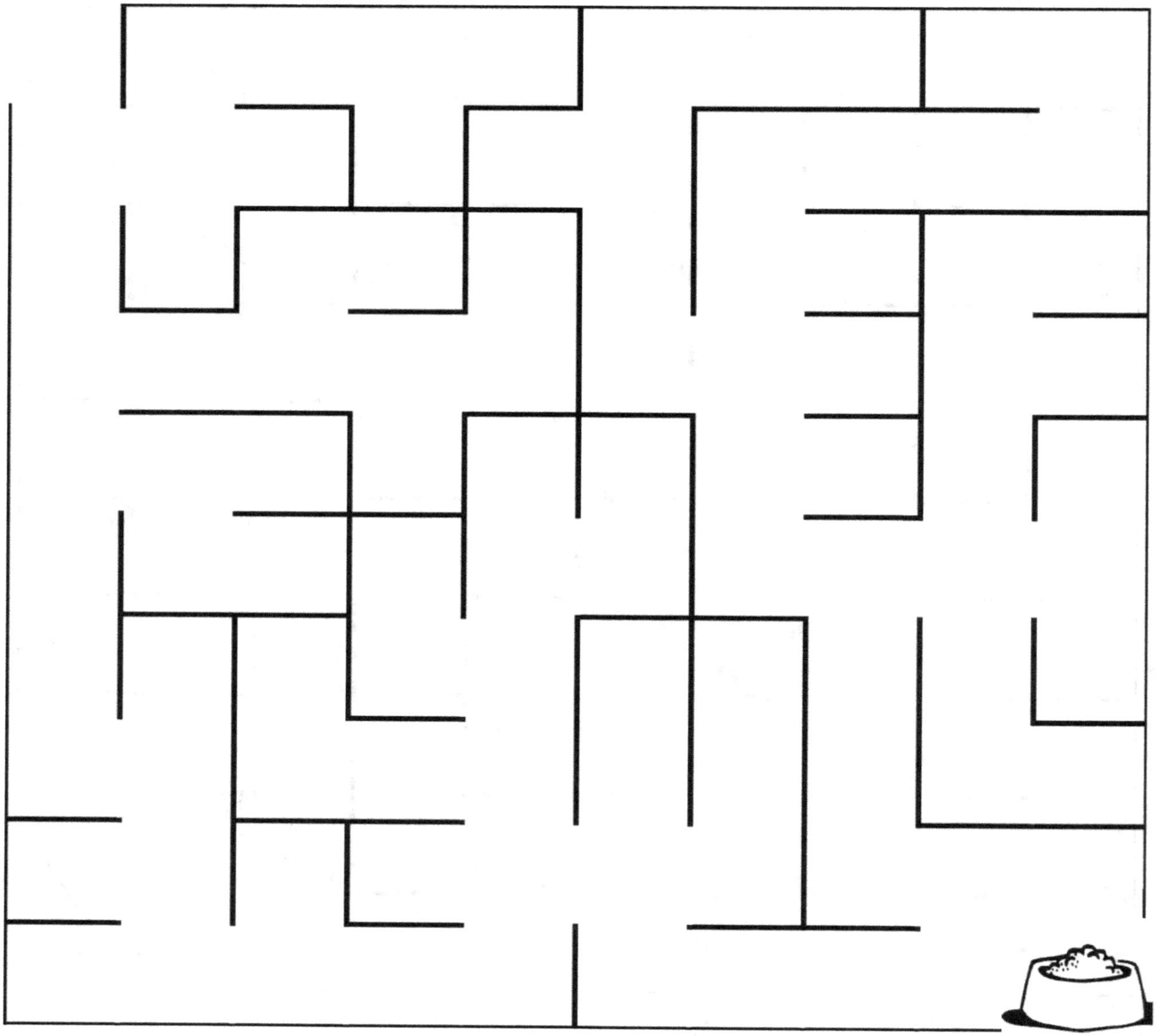

Puzzle 2 - Beginner

Mommy Cindy lost her baby pup Cece in the park. Help her to find baby Cece now.

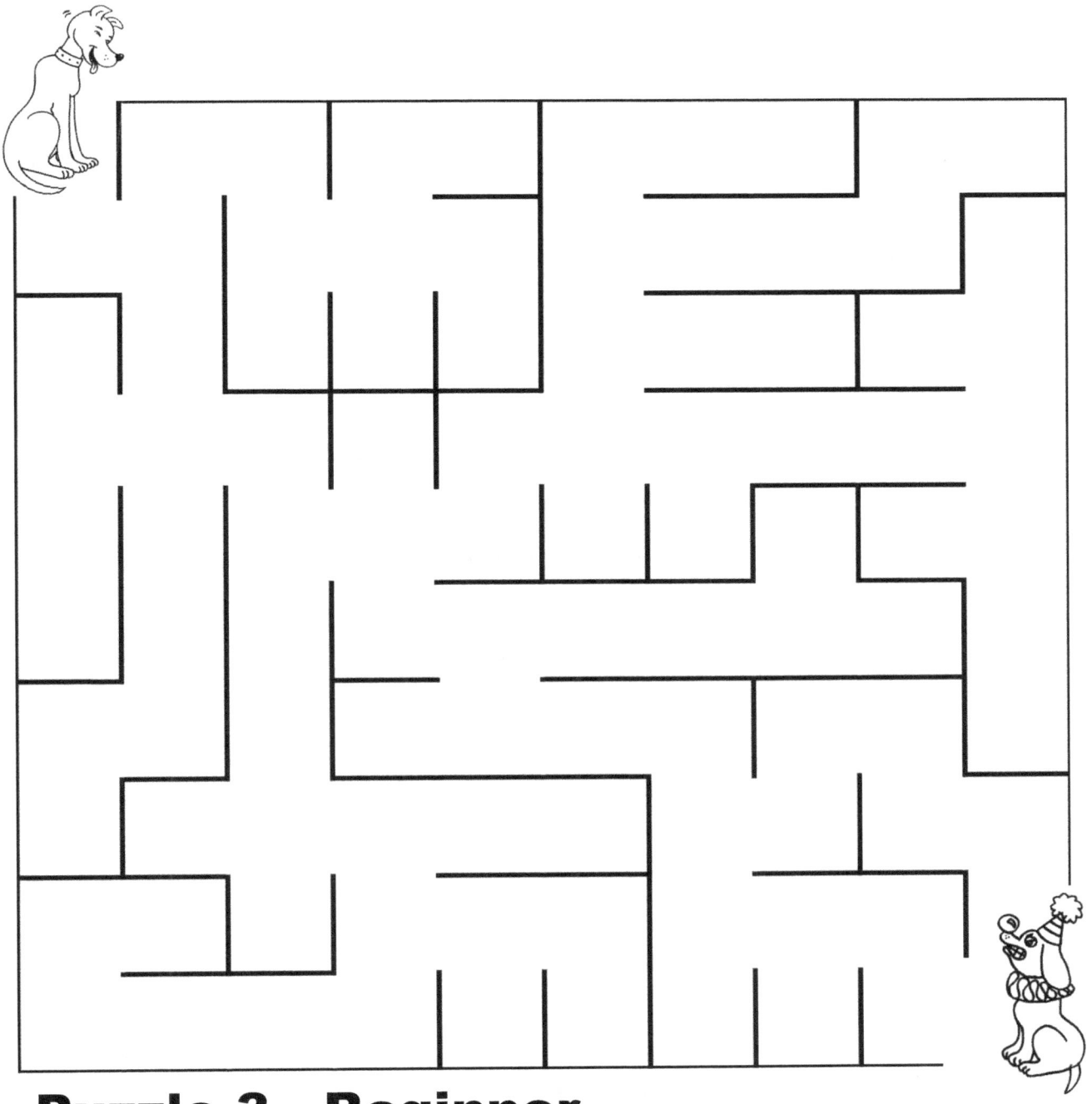

Puzzle 3 - Beginner

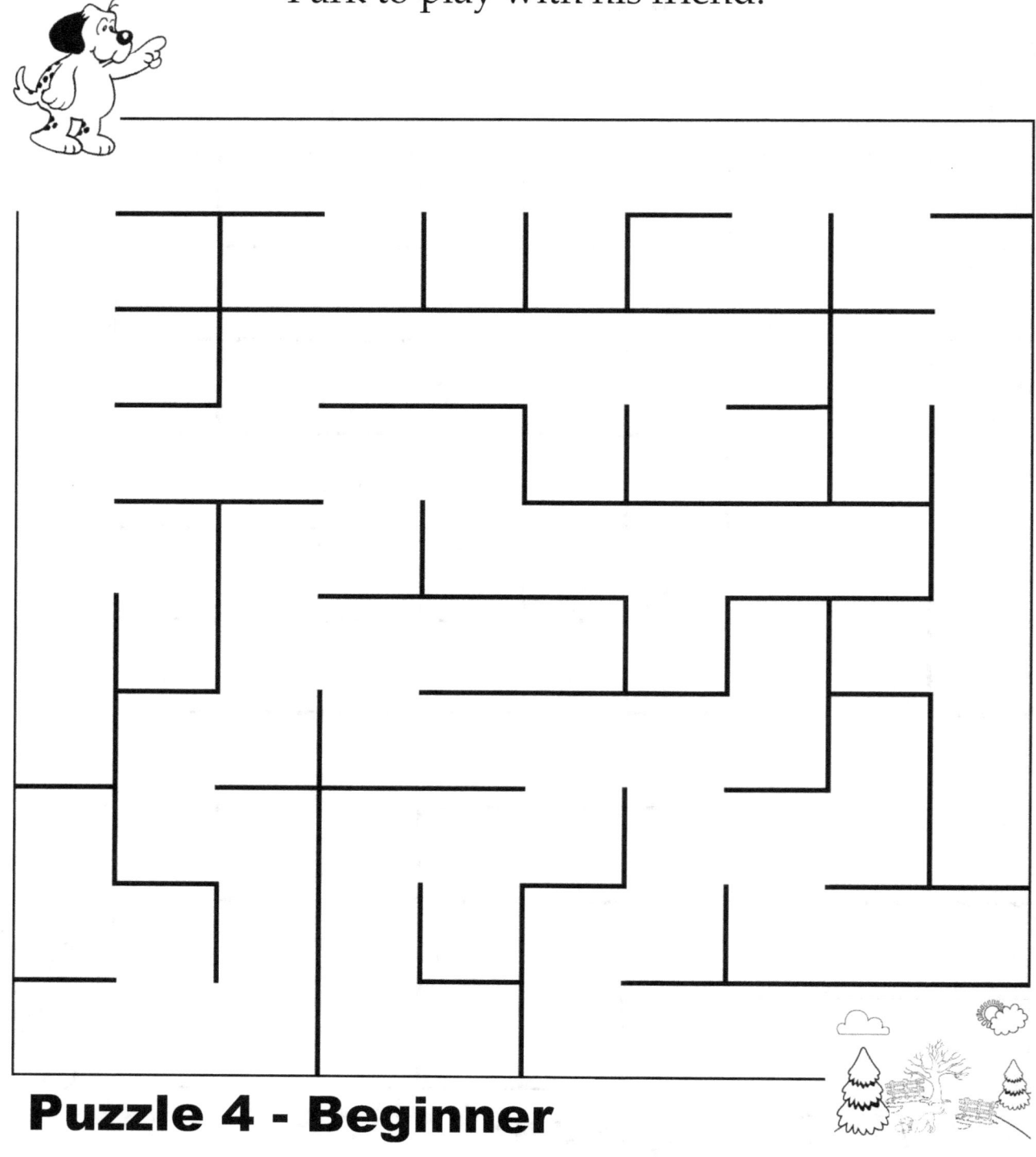

Hey You! Take Bambi to the Park to play with his friend.

Puzzle 4 - Beginner

Puzzle 5 - Beginner

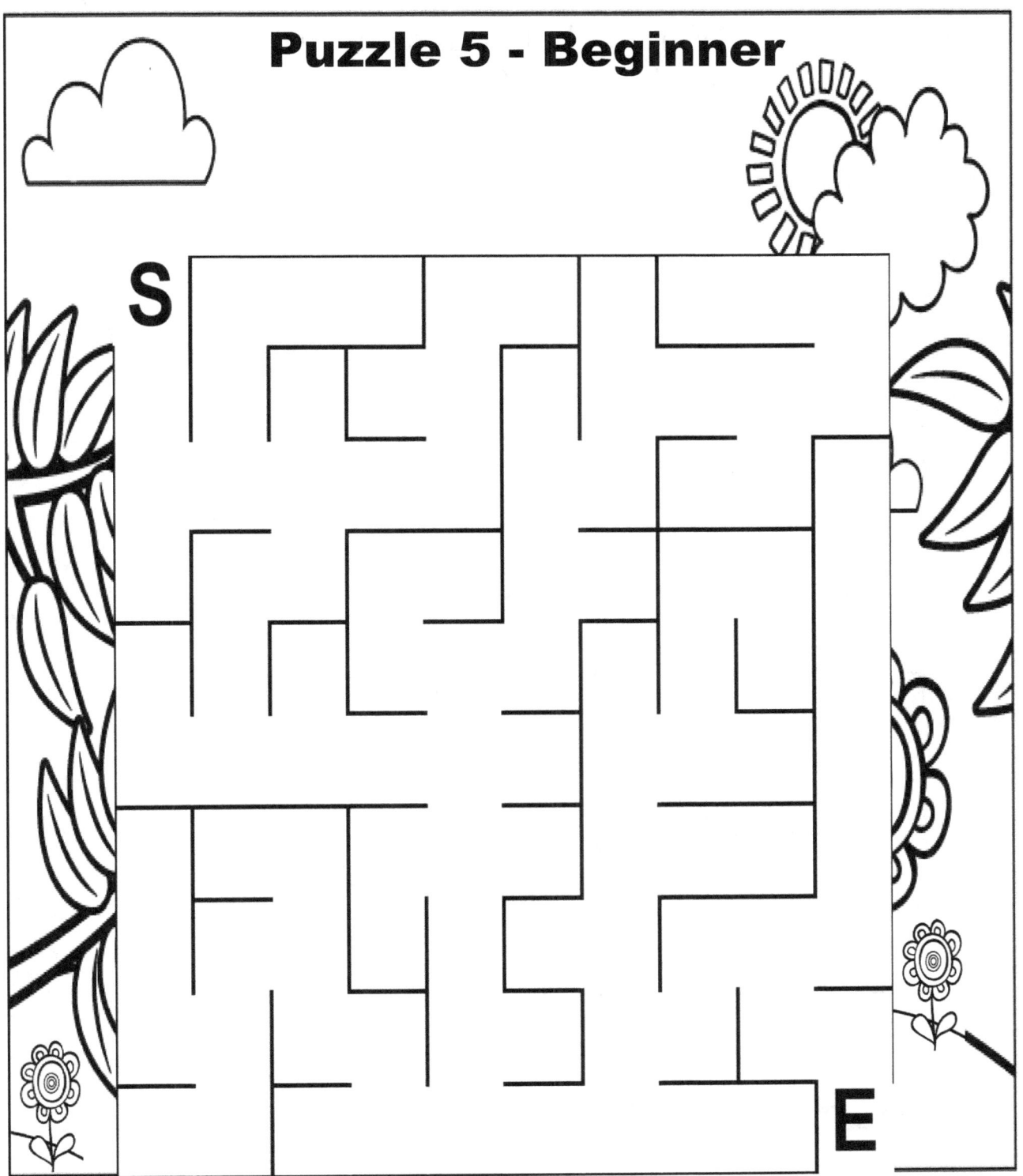

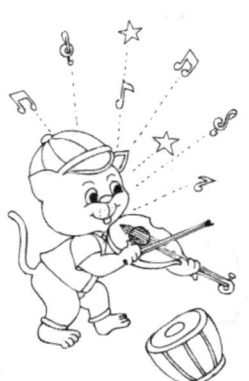

Will you help Bugs dance
to the beat of the music?

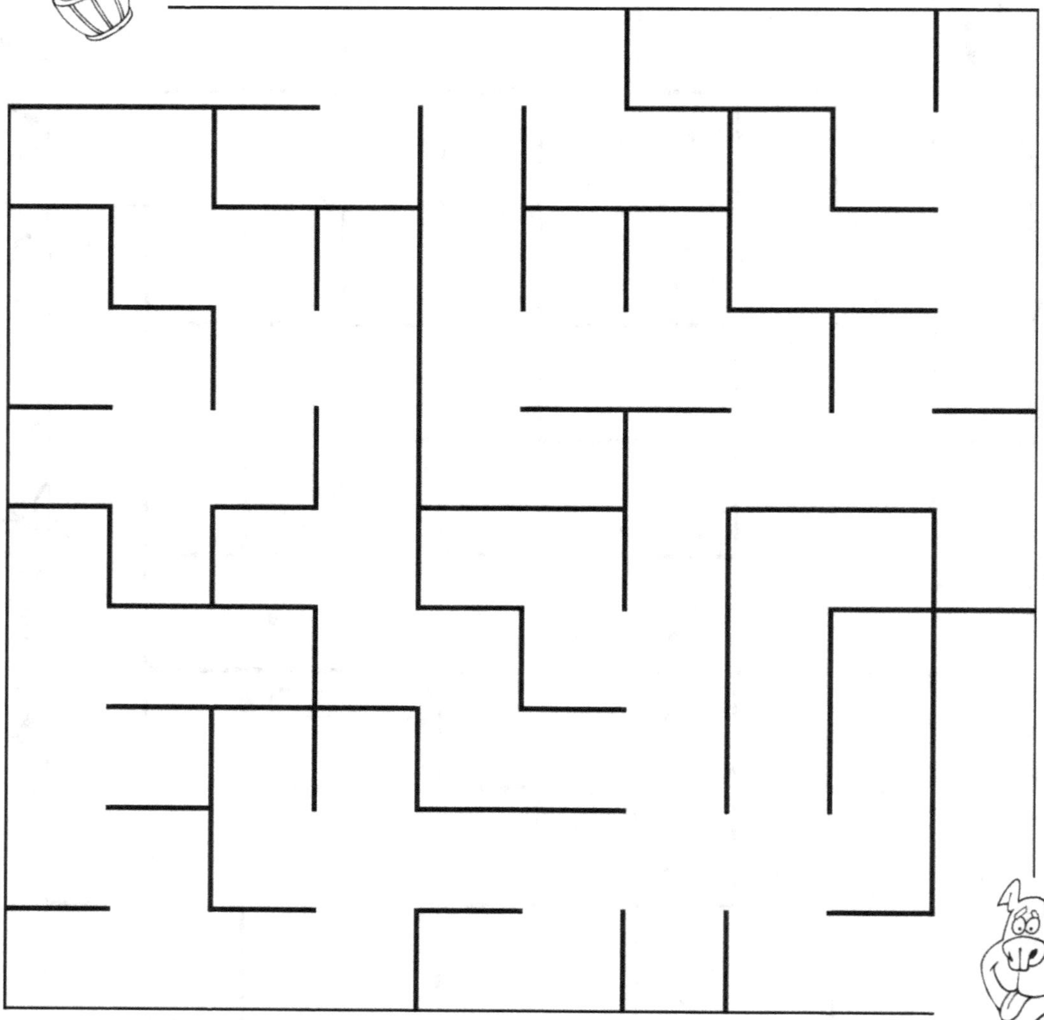

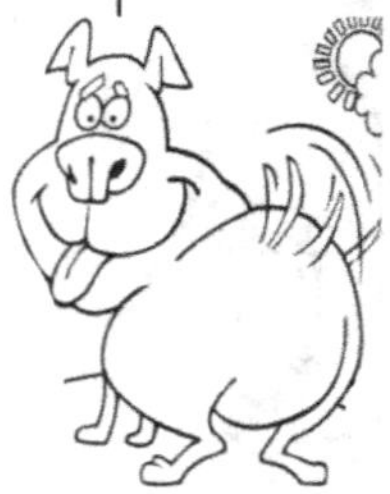

Puzzle 6 - Beginner

Little Santa is bring a gift for Scottie. Help him find Scottie who is waiting.

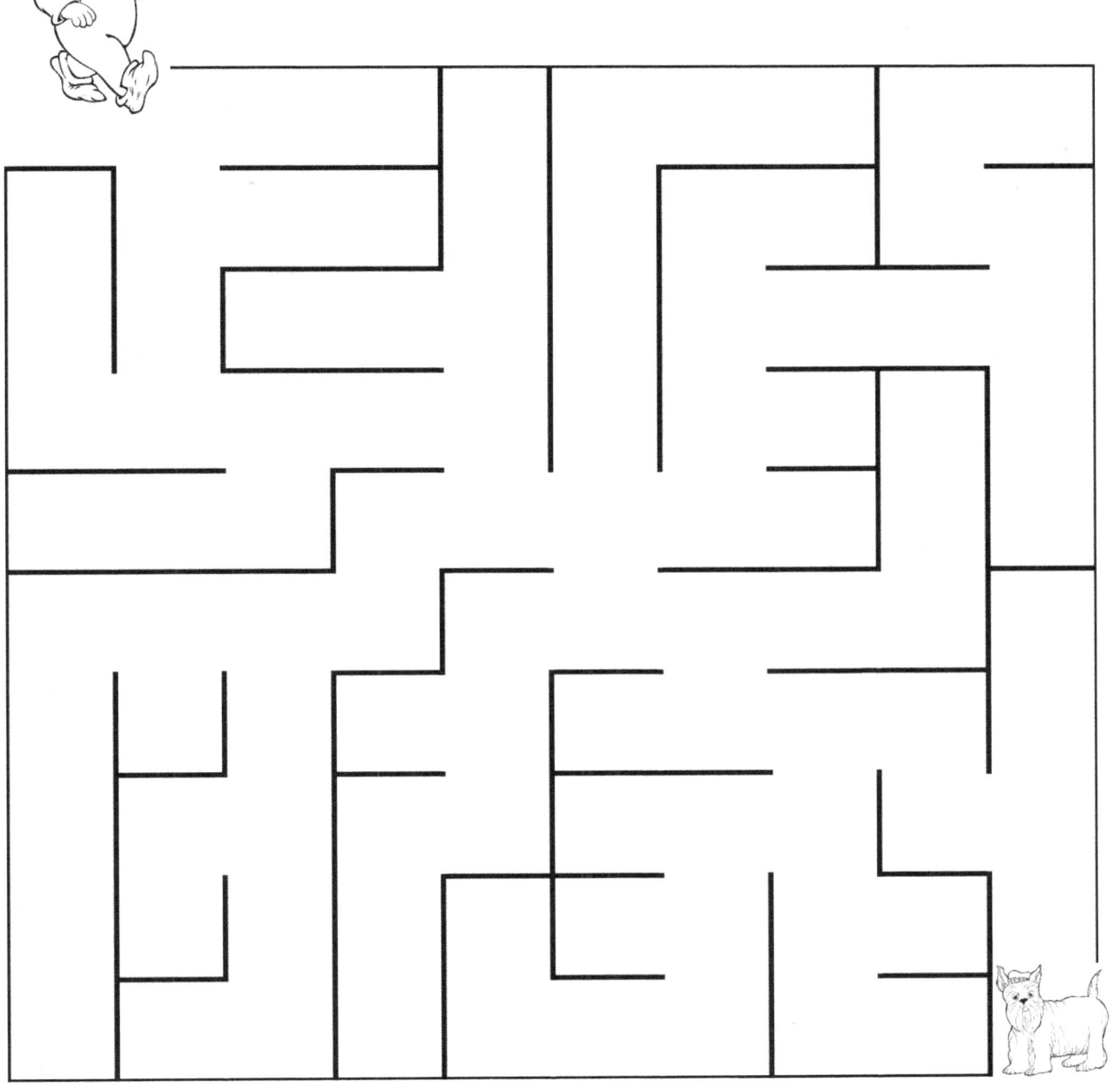

Puzzle 7 - Beginner

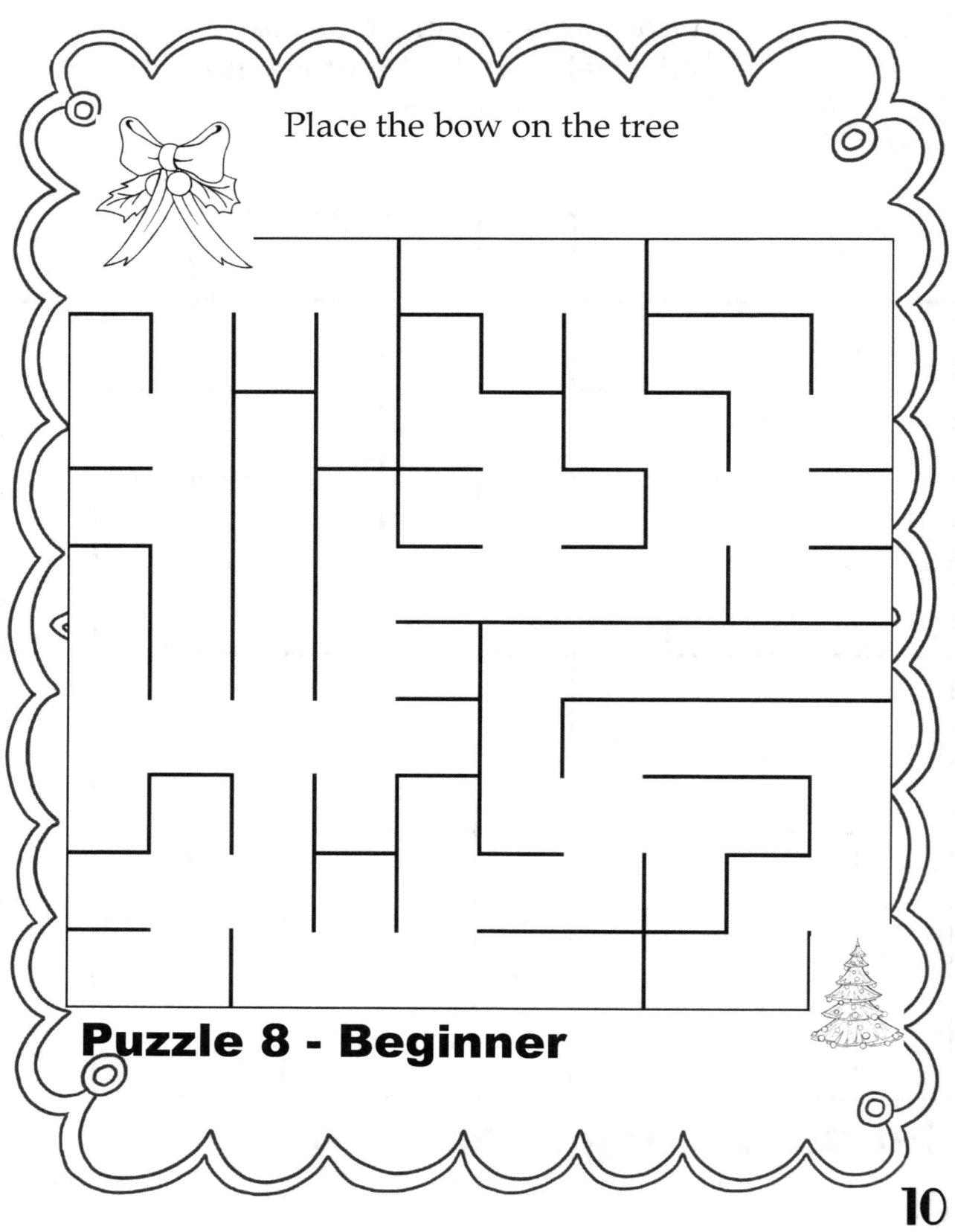

Place the bow on the tree

Puzzle 8 - Beginner

Take a look at the gift Santa left you for Christmas

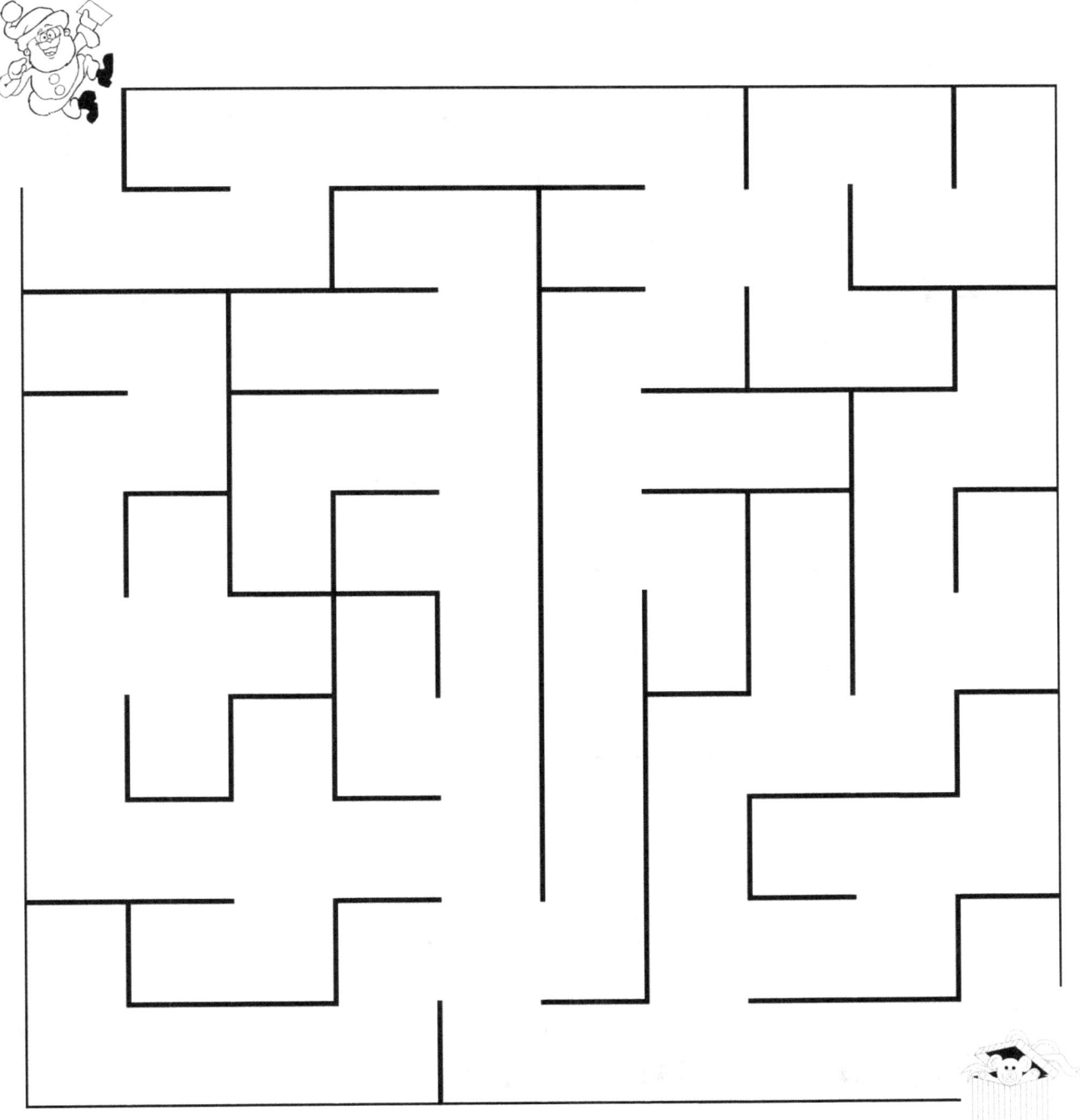

Puzzle 9 - Beginner

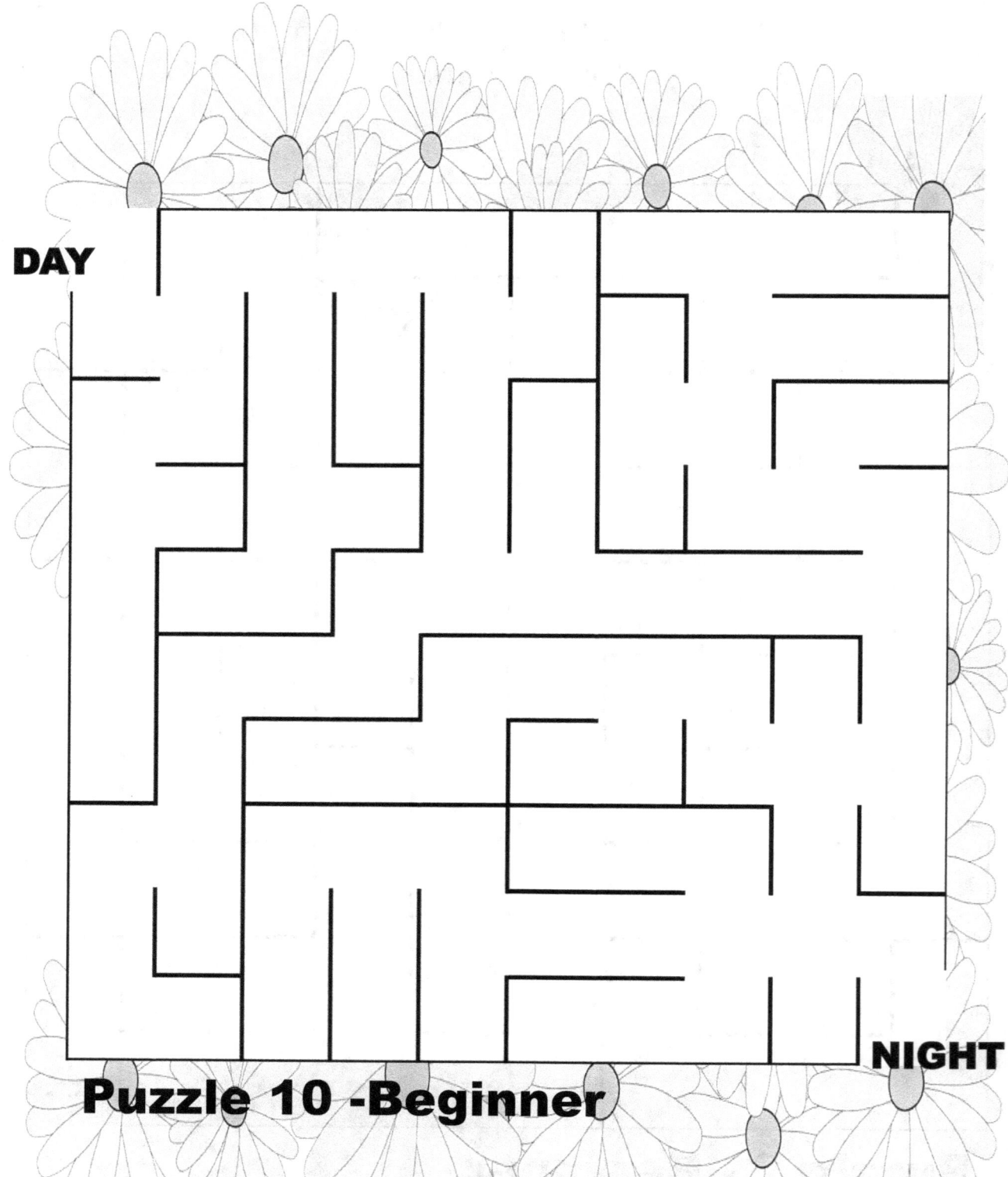

Puzzle 10 - Beginner

Christmas

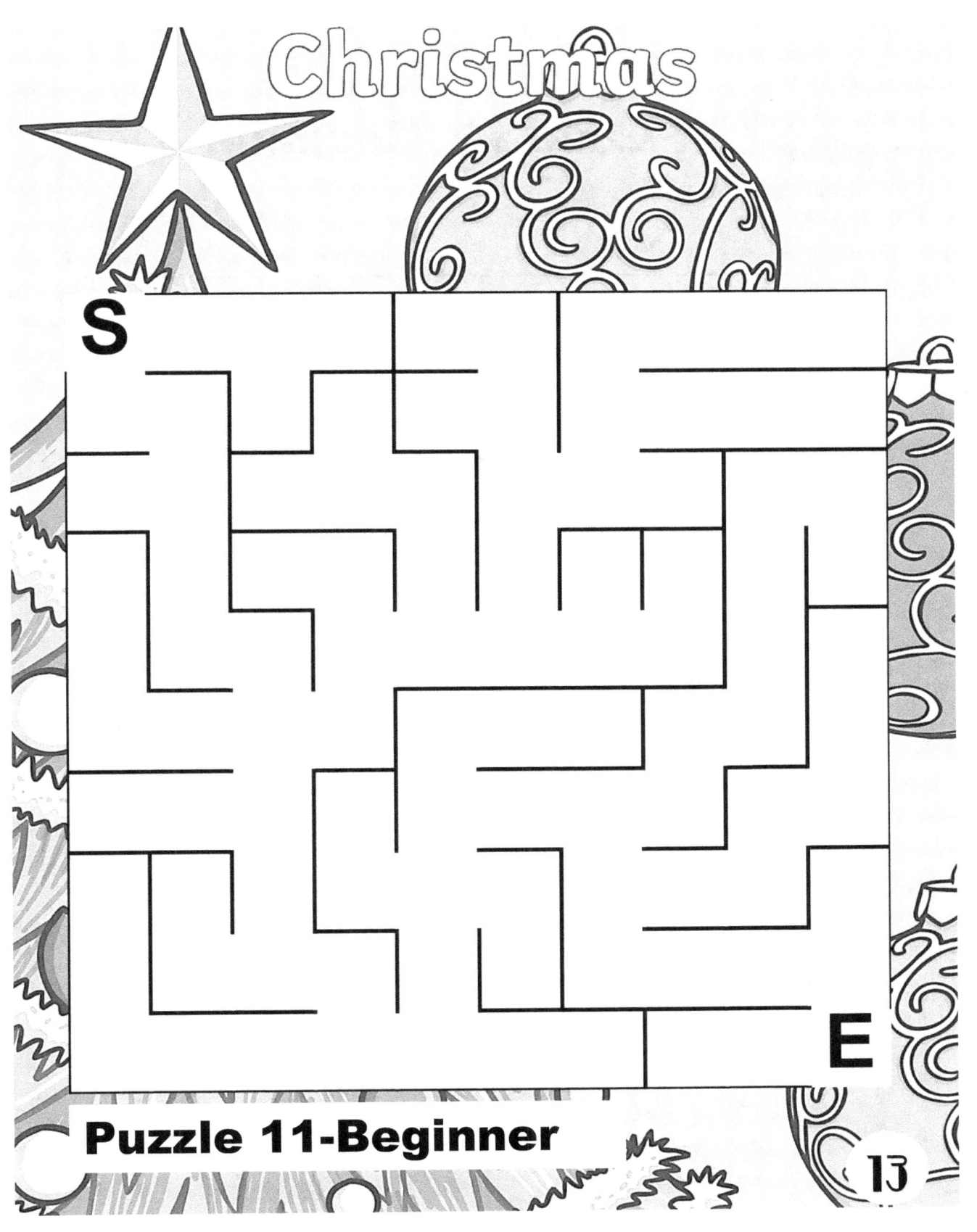

Puzzle 11-Beginner

Under the Sea
Puzzle 12 - Beginner

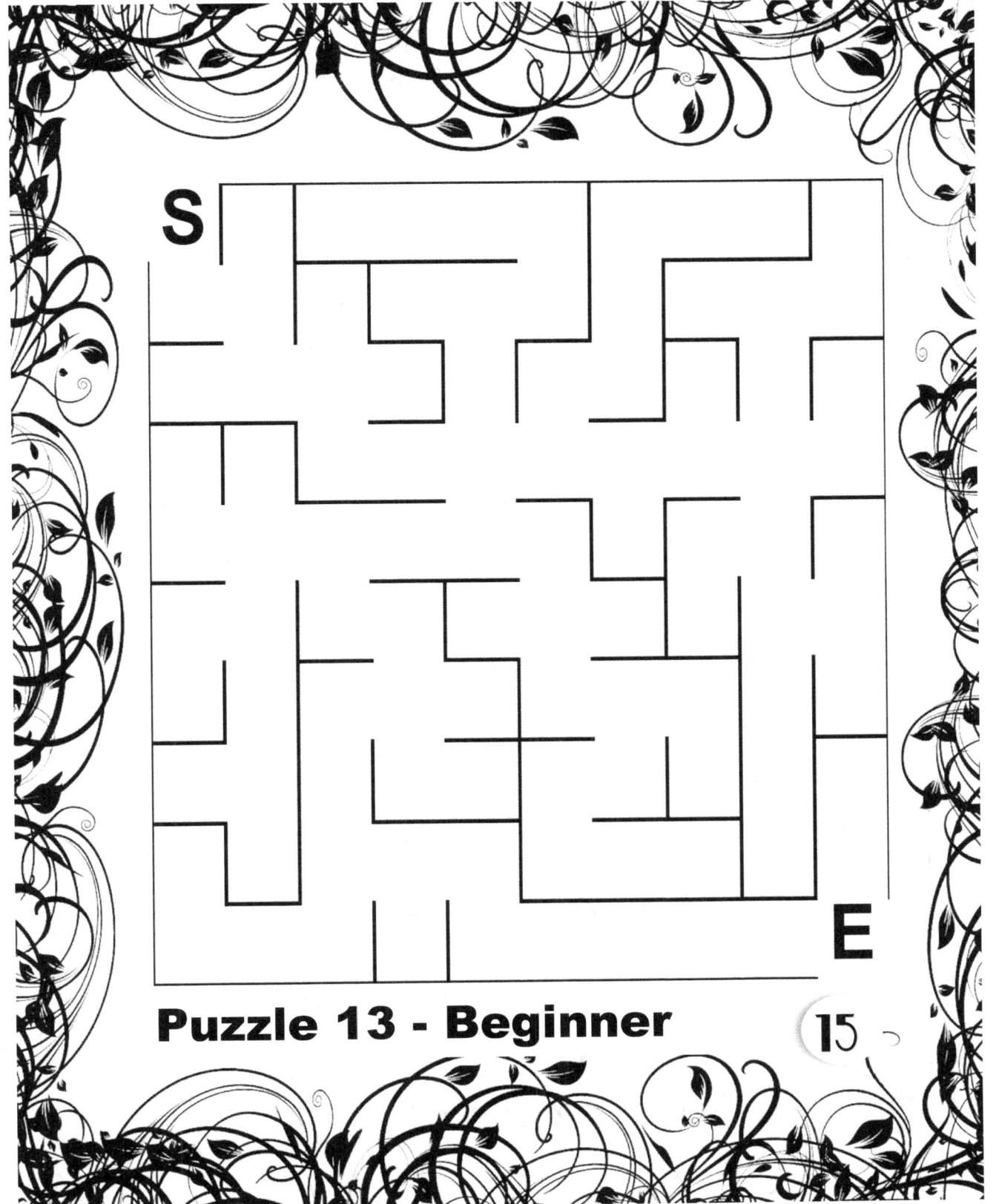

Puzzle 13 - Beginner

Santa is bringing you goodies

Puzzle 14 - Beginner

Puzzle 15 - Beginner

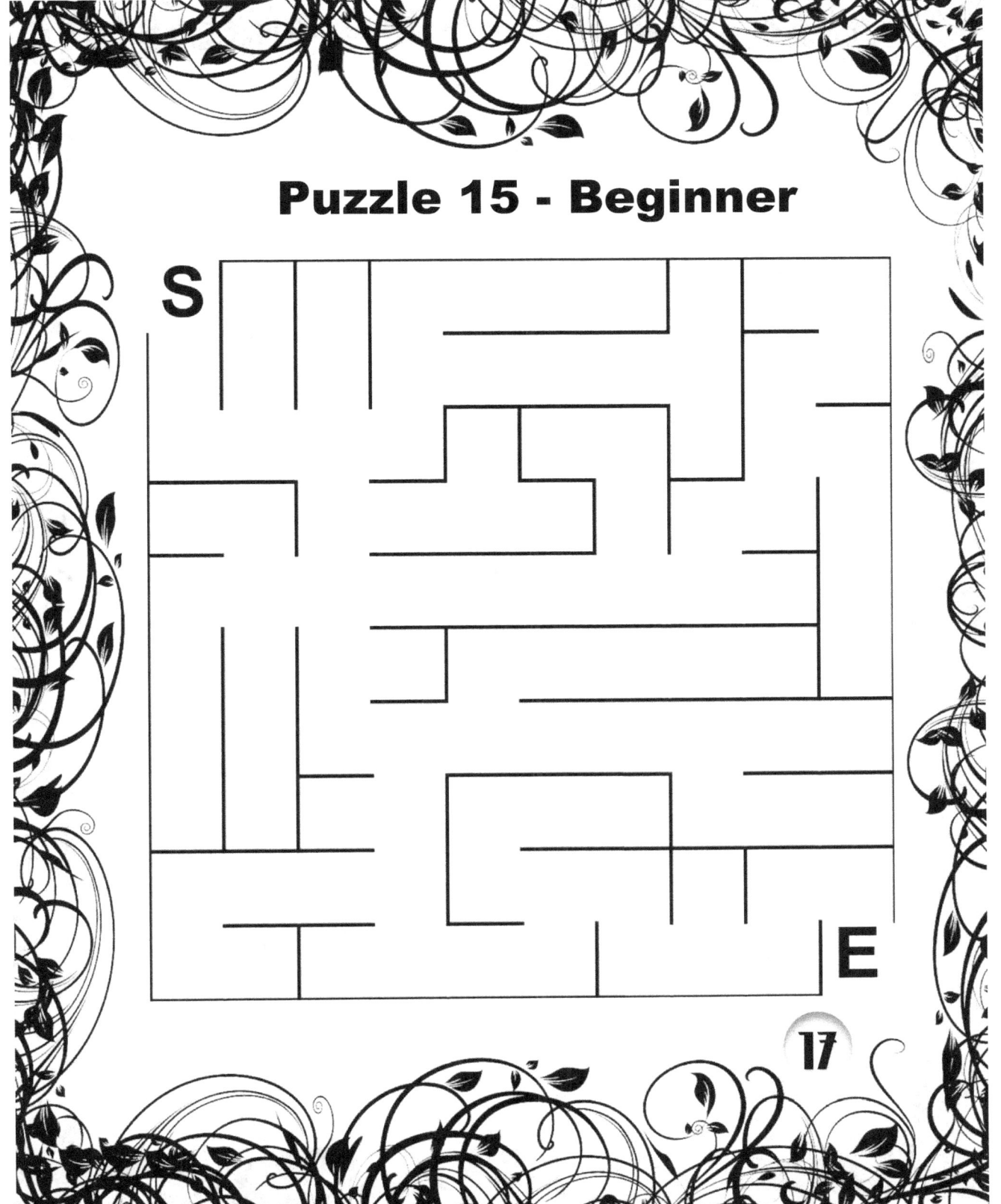

Puzzle 16 - Easy

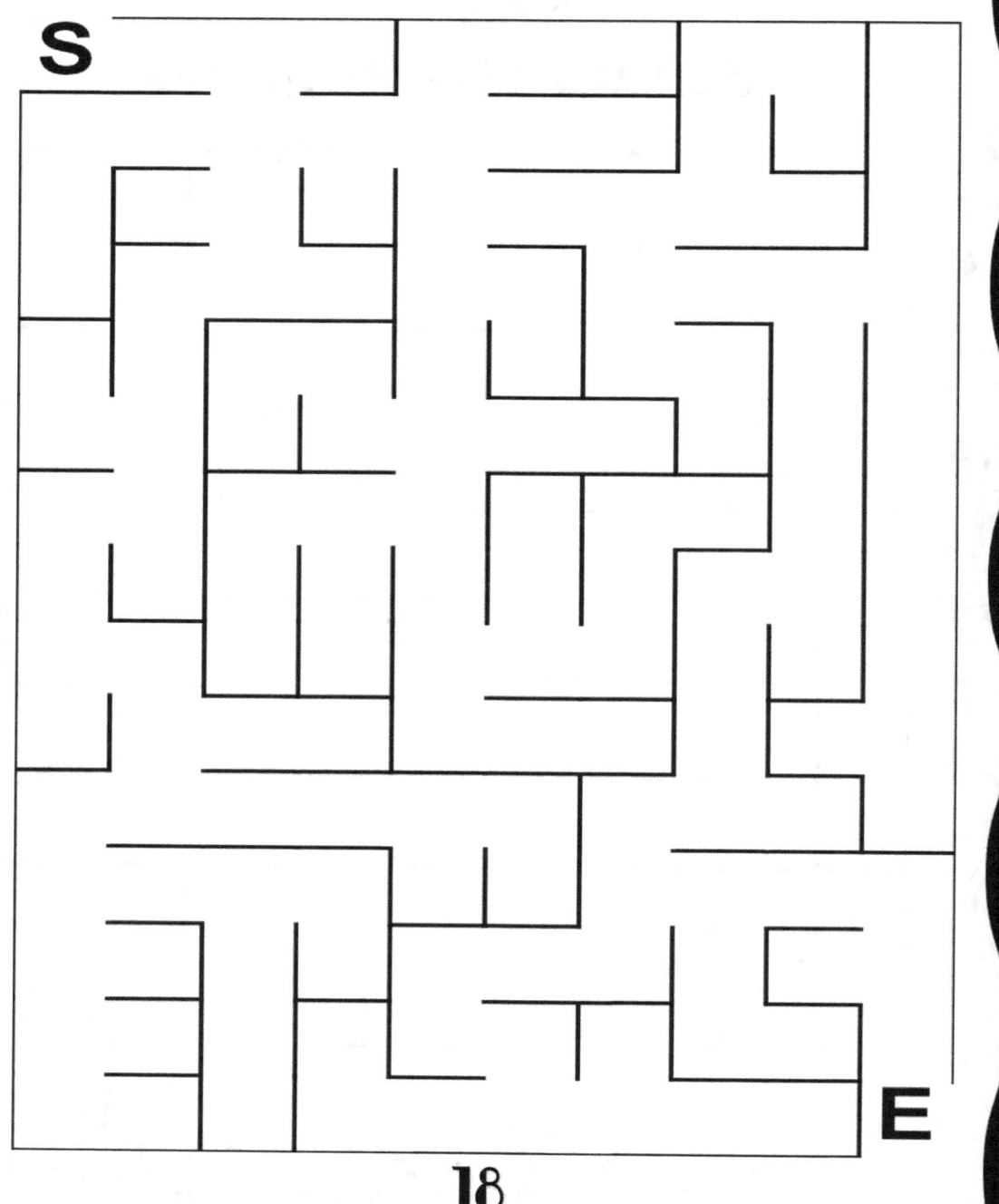

18

Add candy to your gift bag

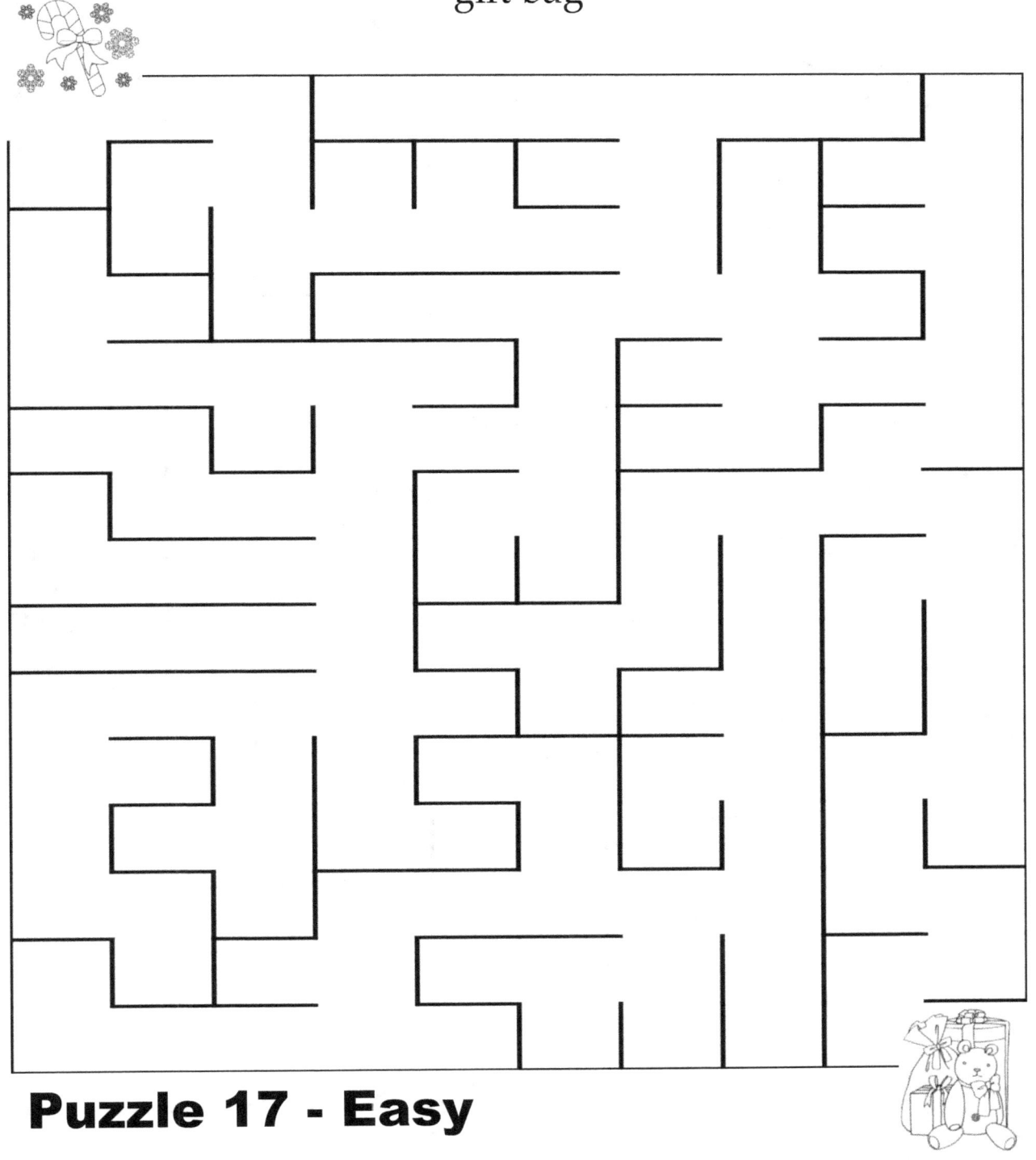

Puzzle 17 - Easy

Puzzle 18 - Easy

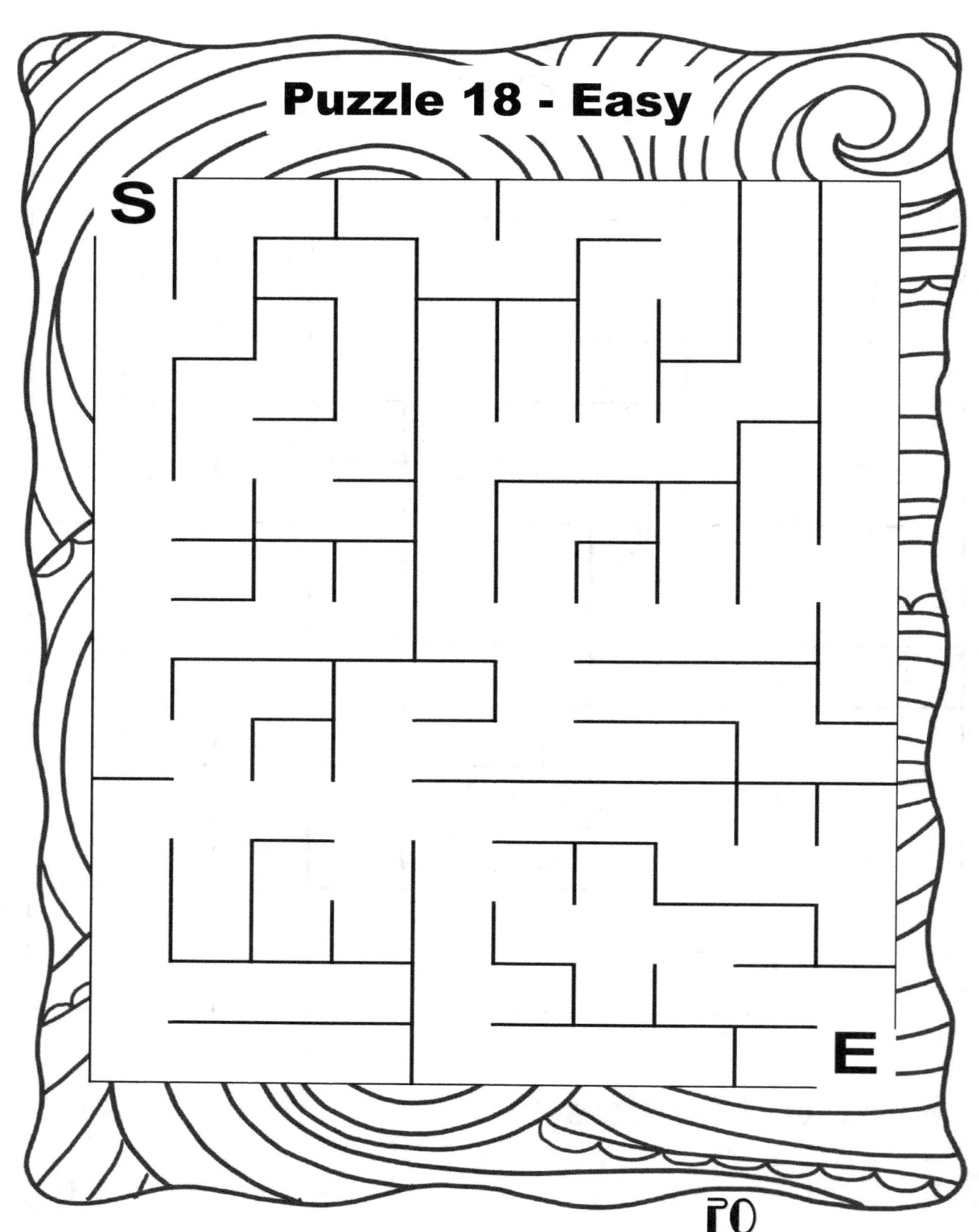

Puzzle 19 - Easy

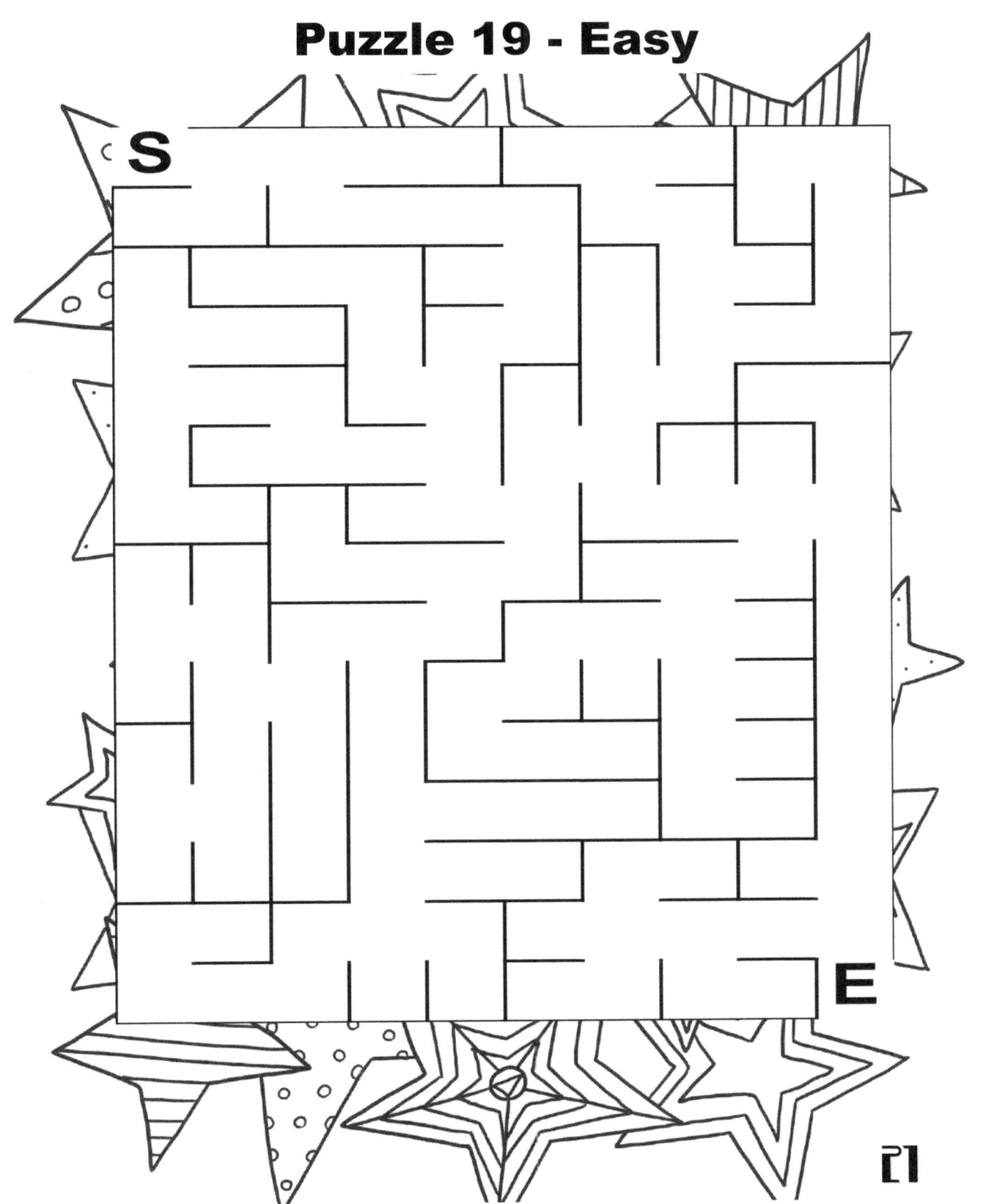

Puzzle 20 - Easy

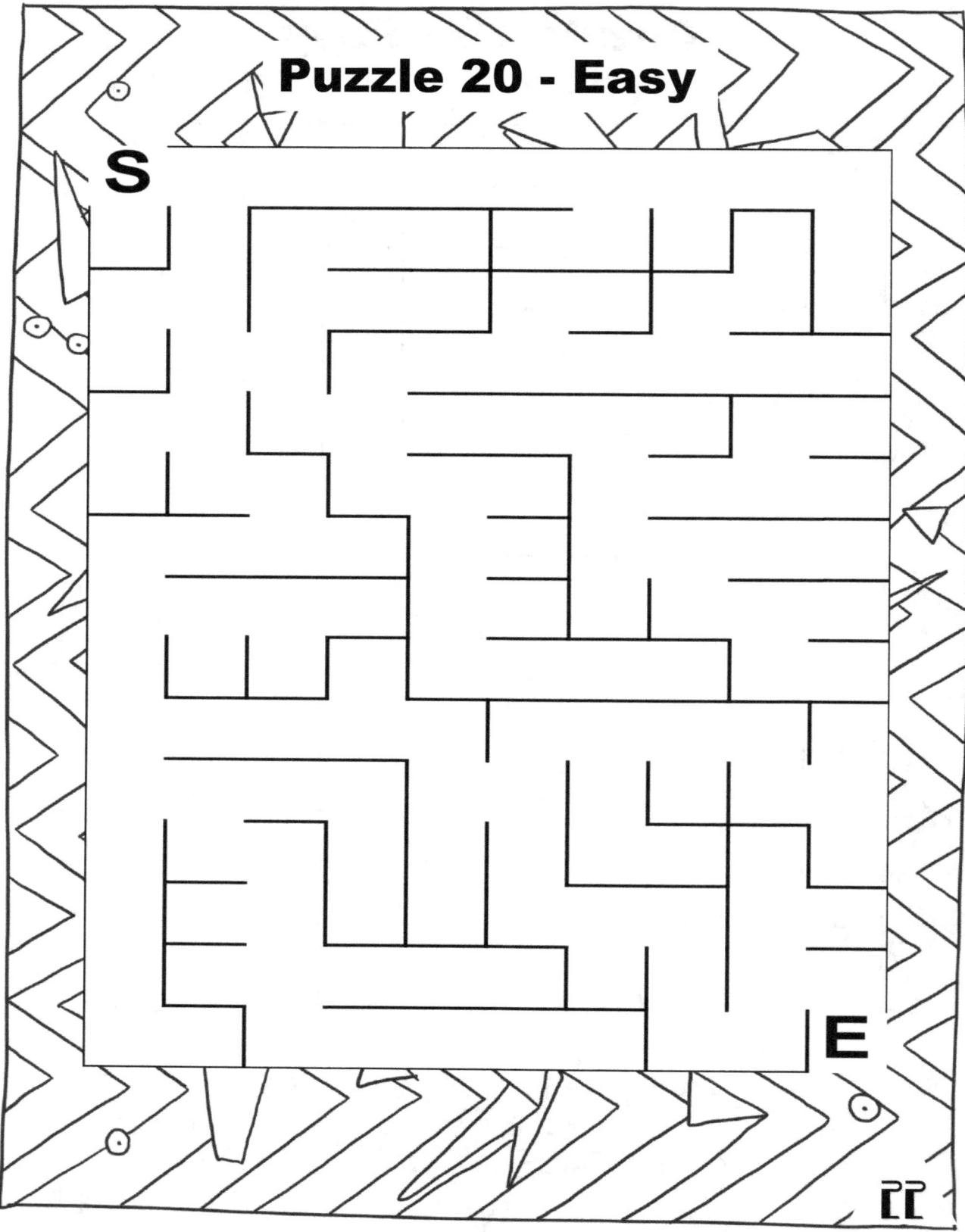

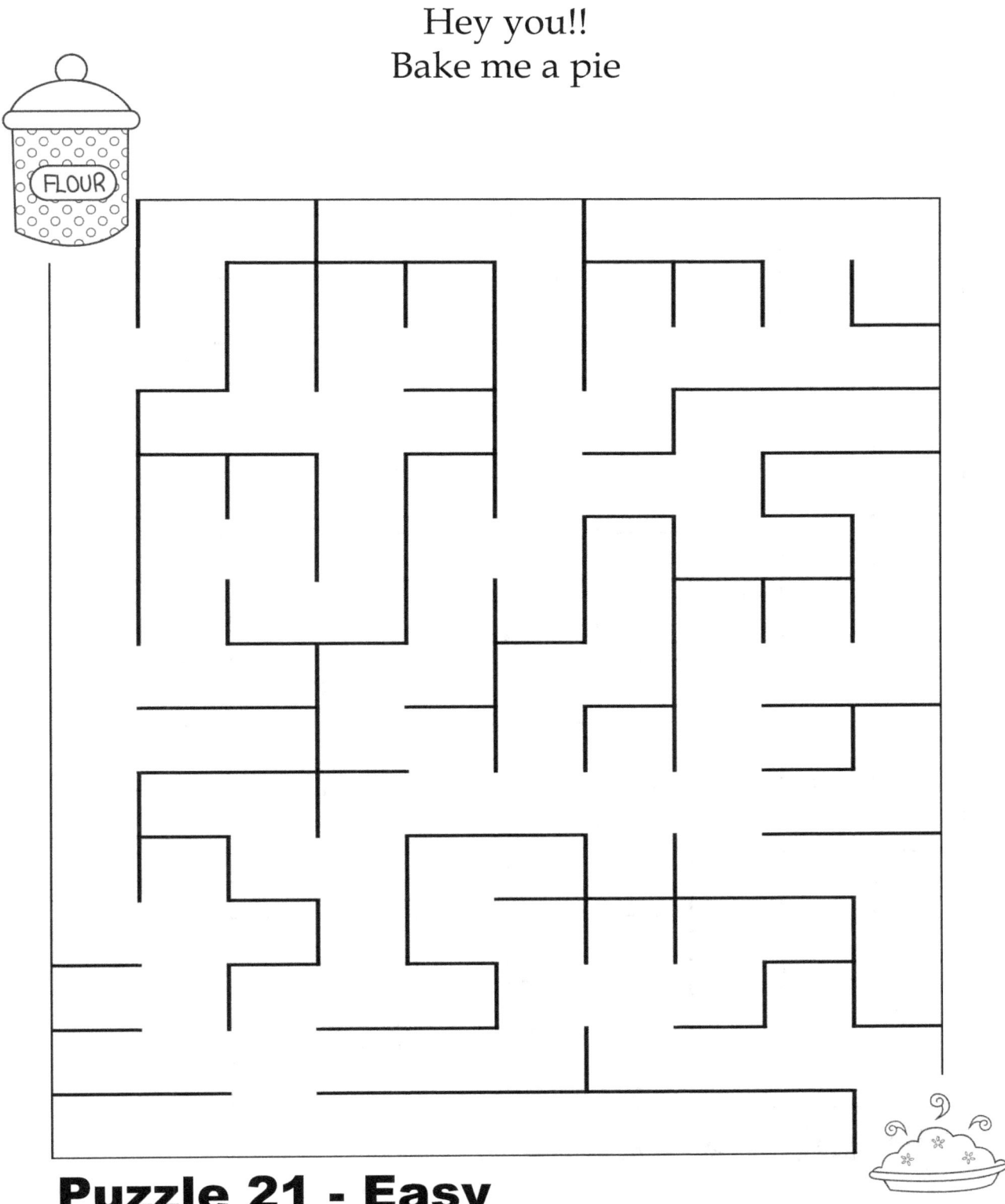

Puzzle 21 - Easy

Baking Essentials

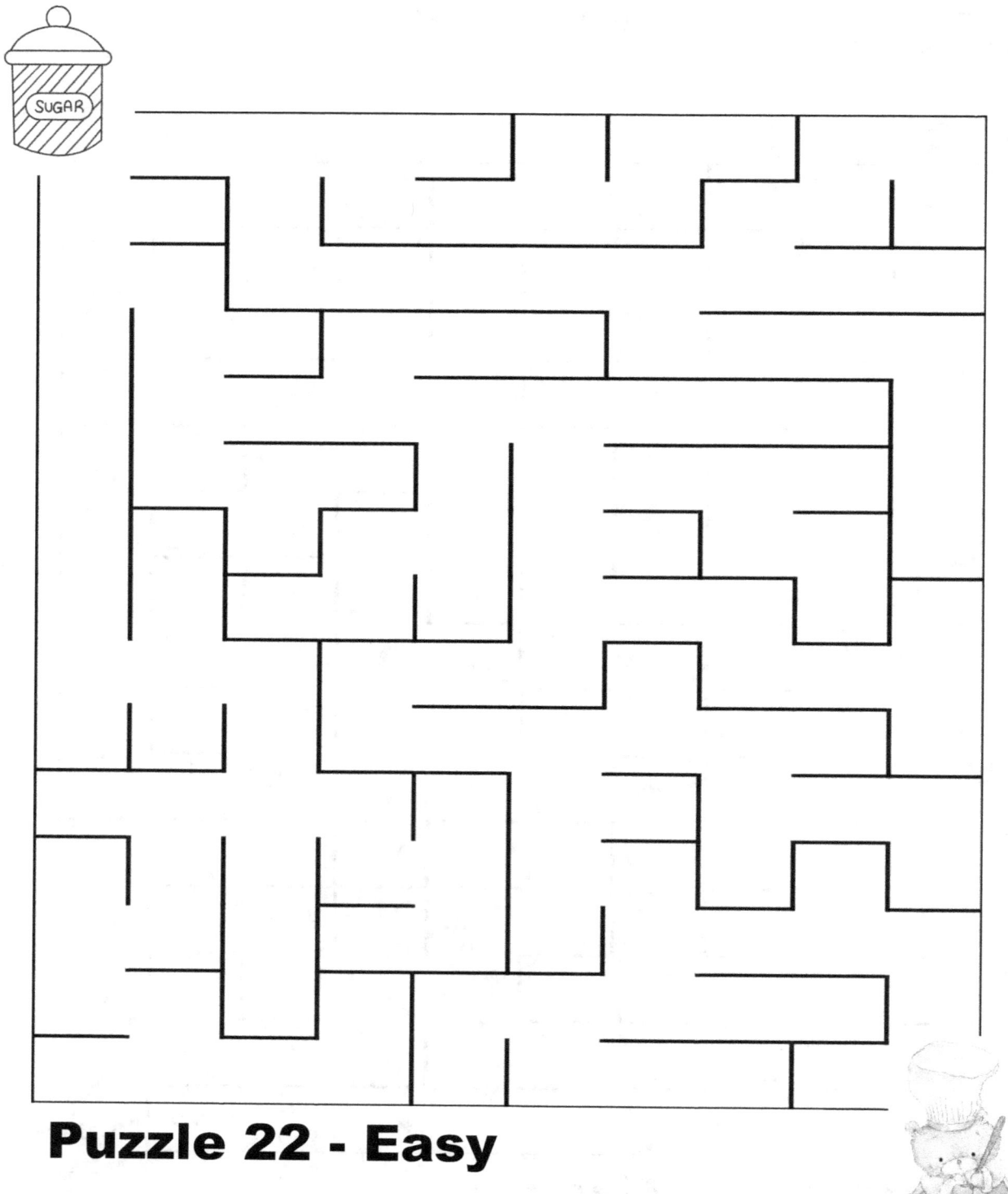

Puzzle 22 - Easy

Summer Fun

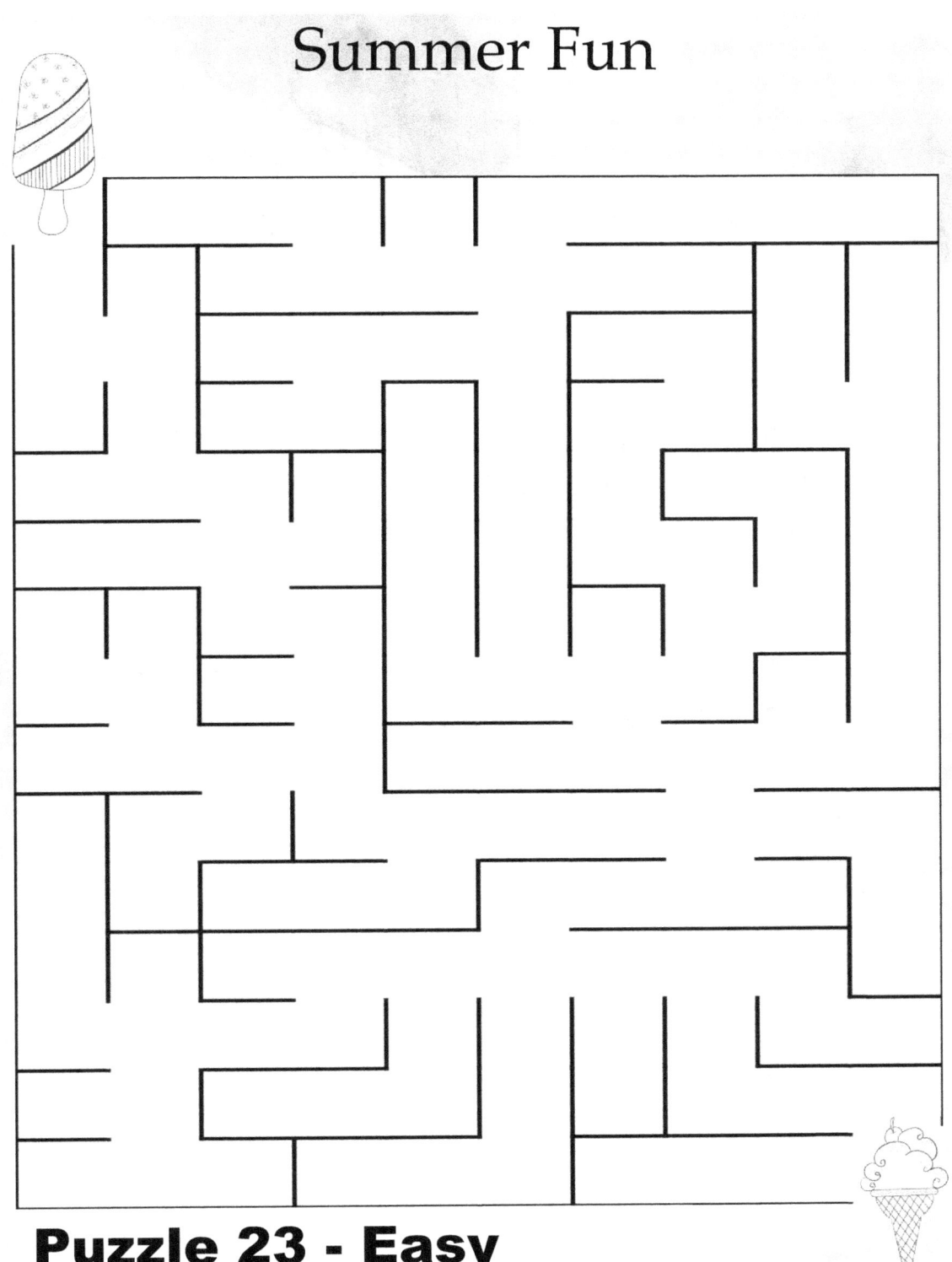

Puzzle 23 - Easy

Spot the Differences

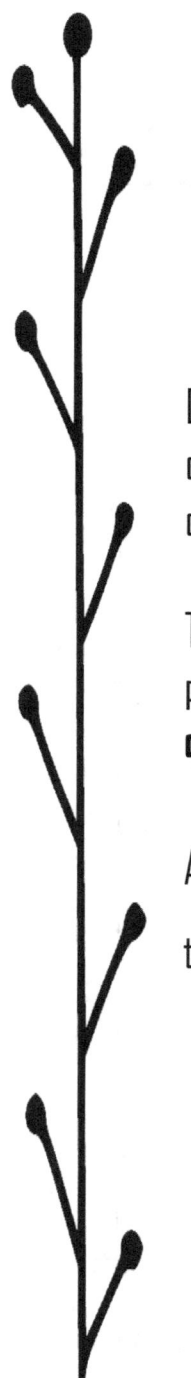

Describing pictures is a useful speaking skill and these sheets can be used as a fun communicative game that is suitable for children who are beginner to elementary level or above.

This game features several lovely illustrations of animals, parks, hobbies and much more - twice! **But there are some differences, can your little detectives spot them all?**

After children have spotted the differences, they can color in their pictures.

Spot the Differences

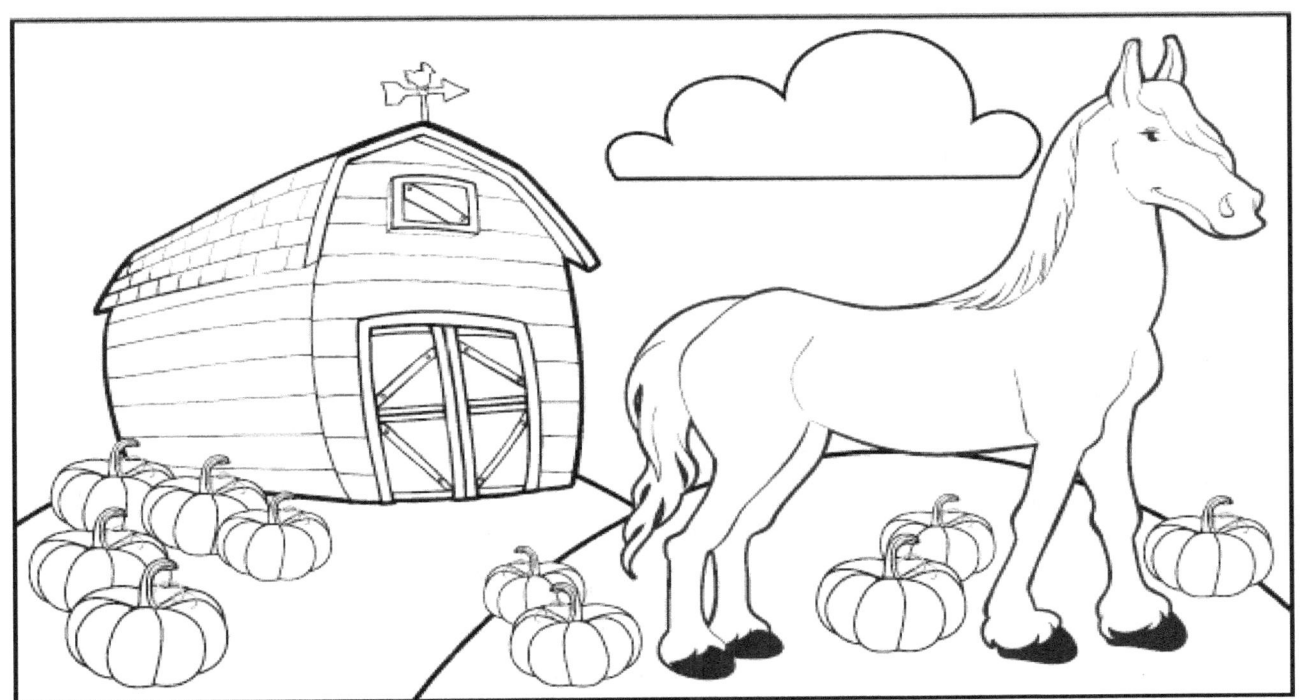

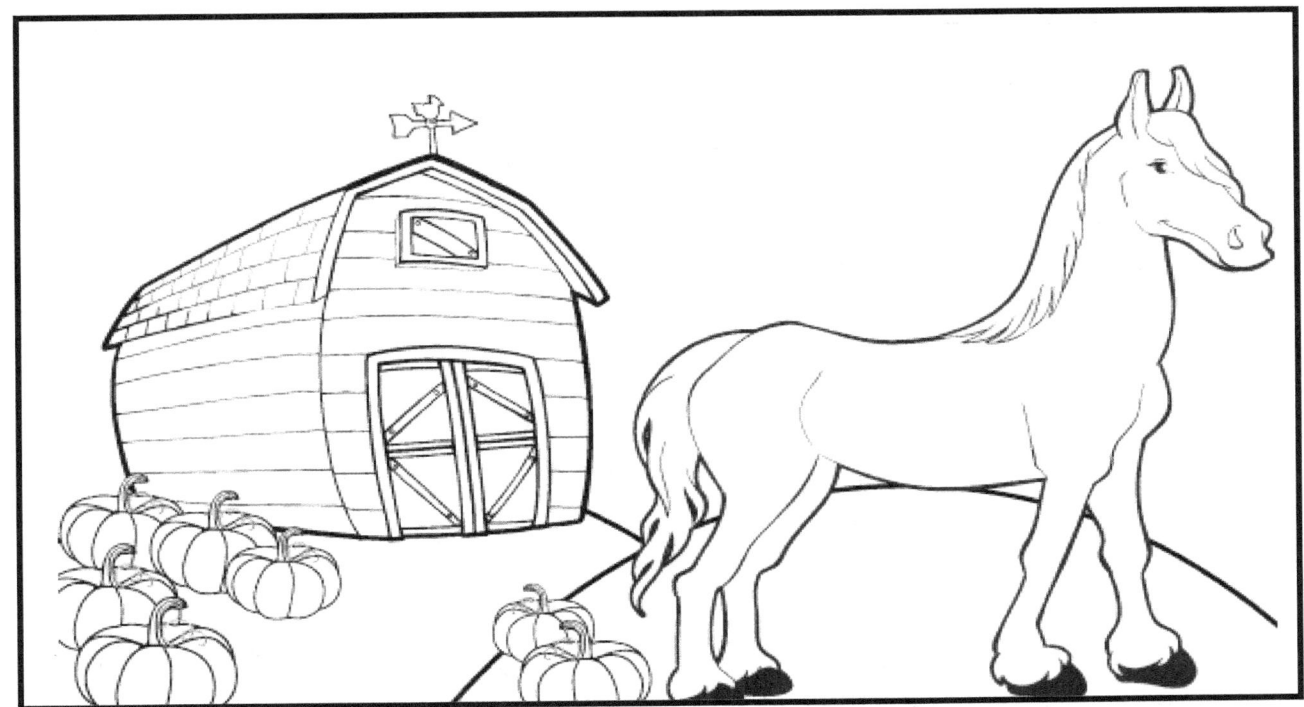

Spot the Differences

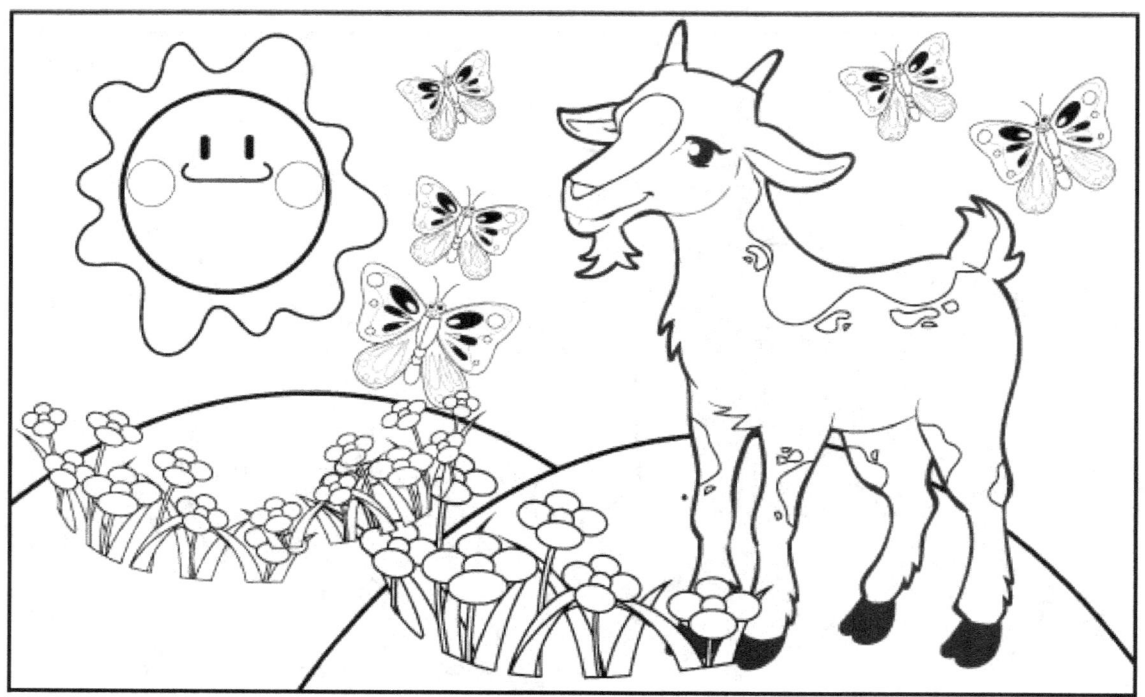

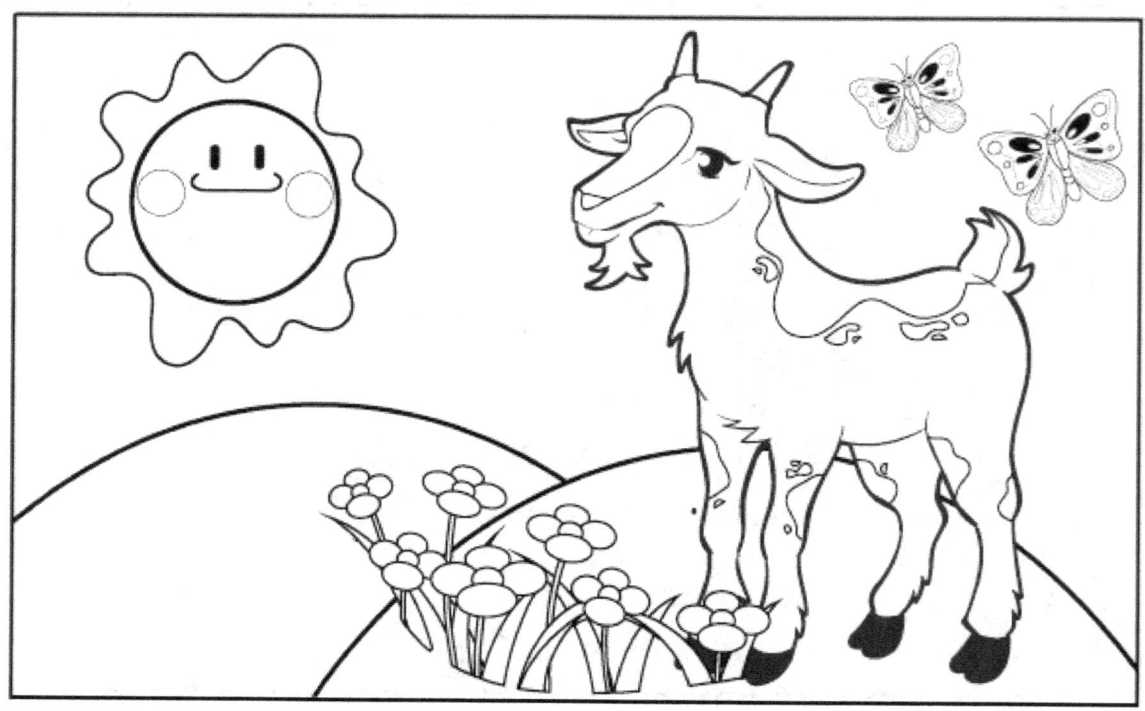

Spot the Differences

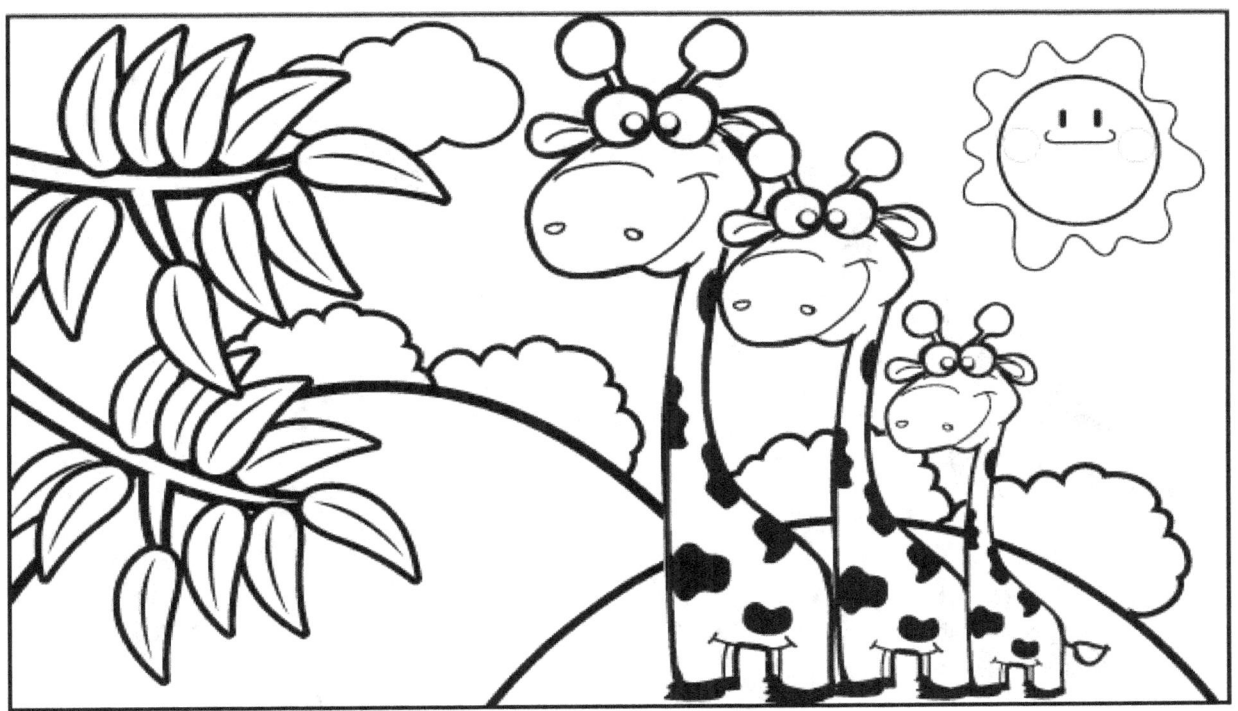

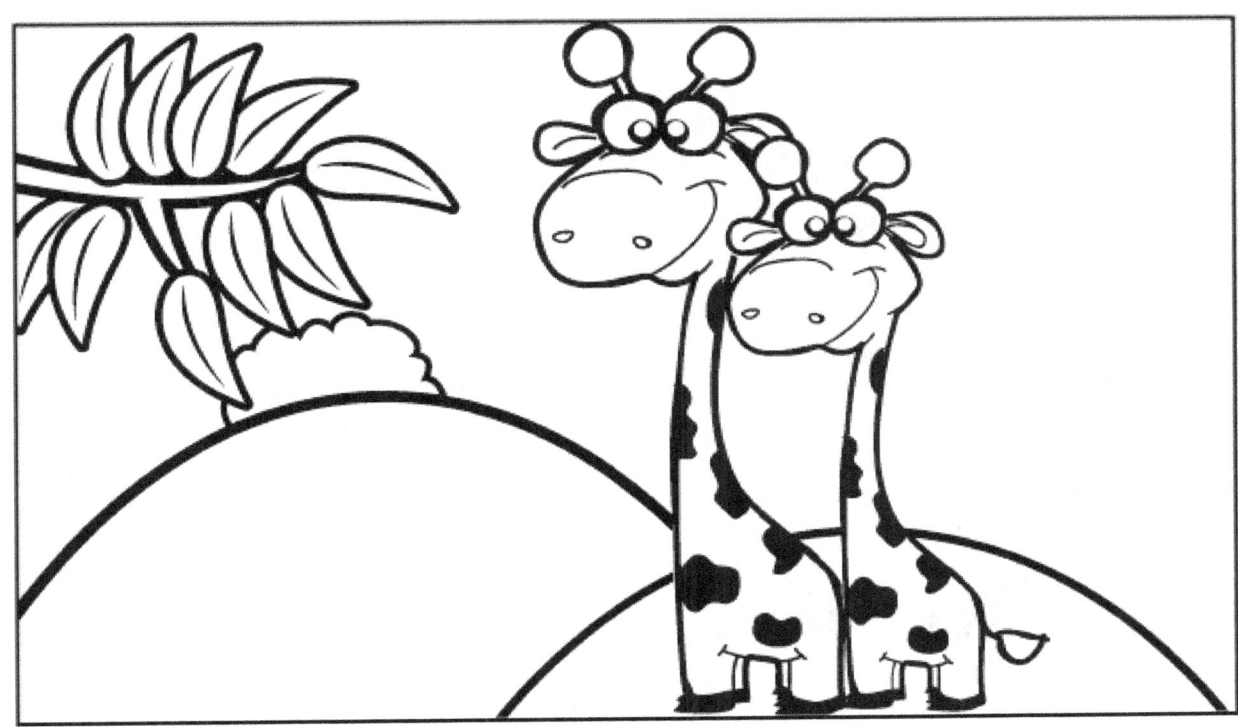

Spot the Differences

30

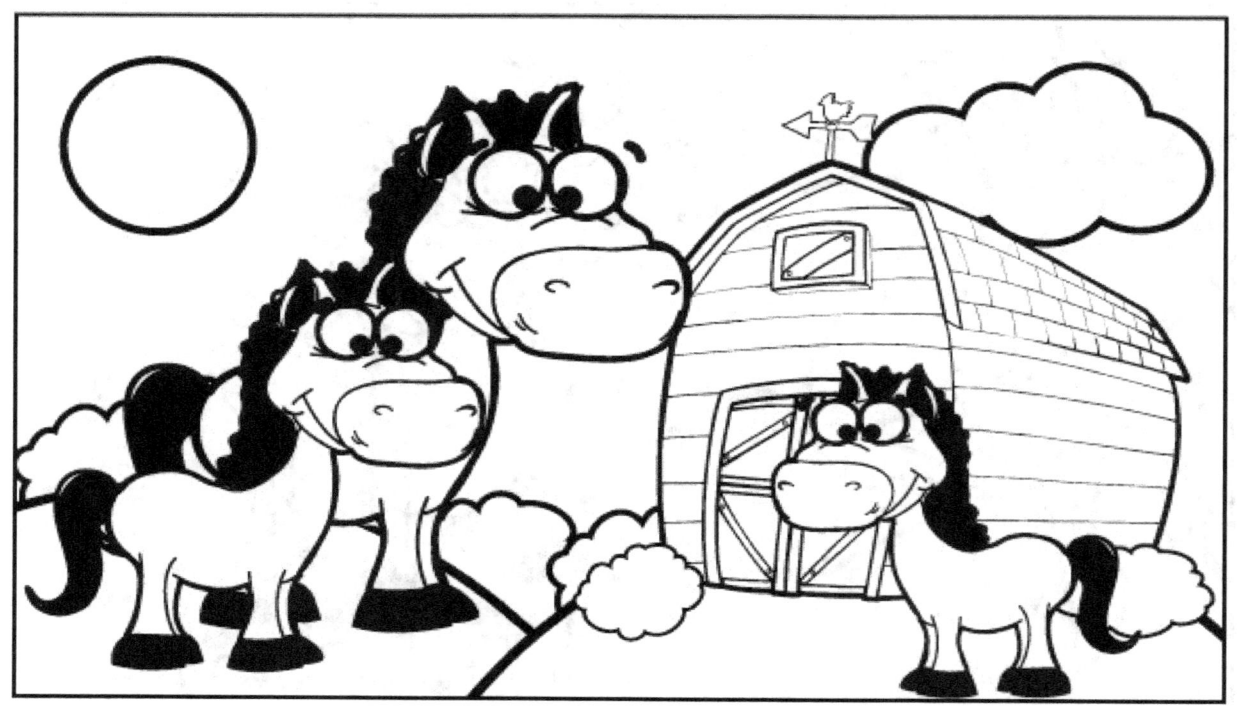

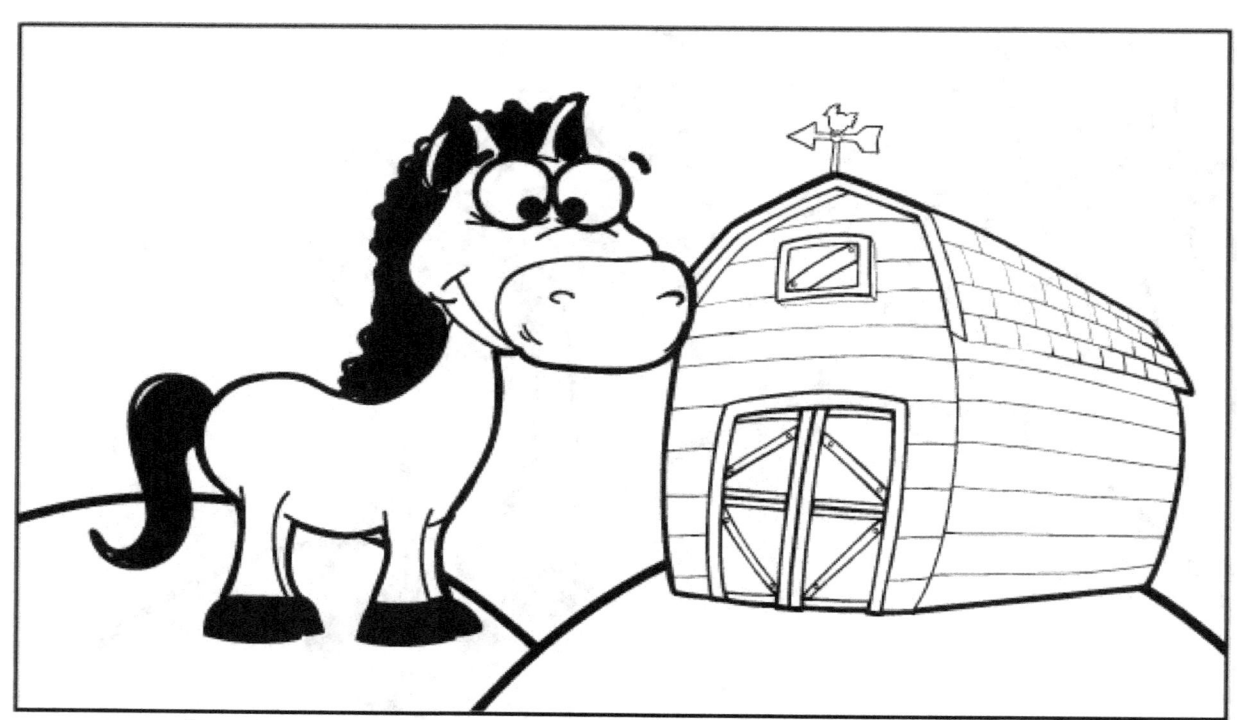

Spot the Differences

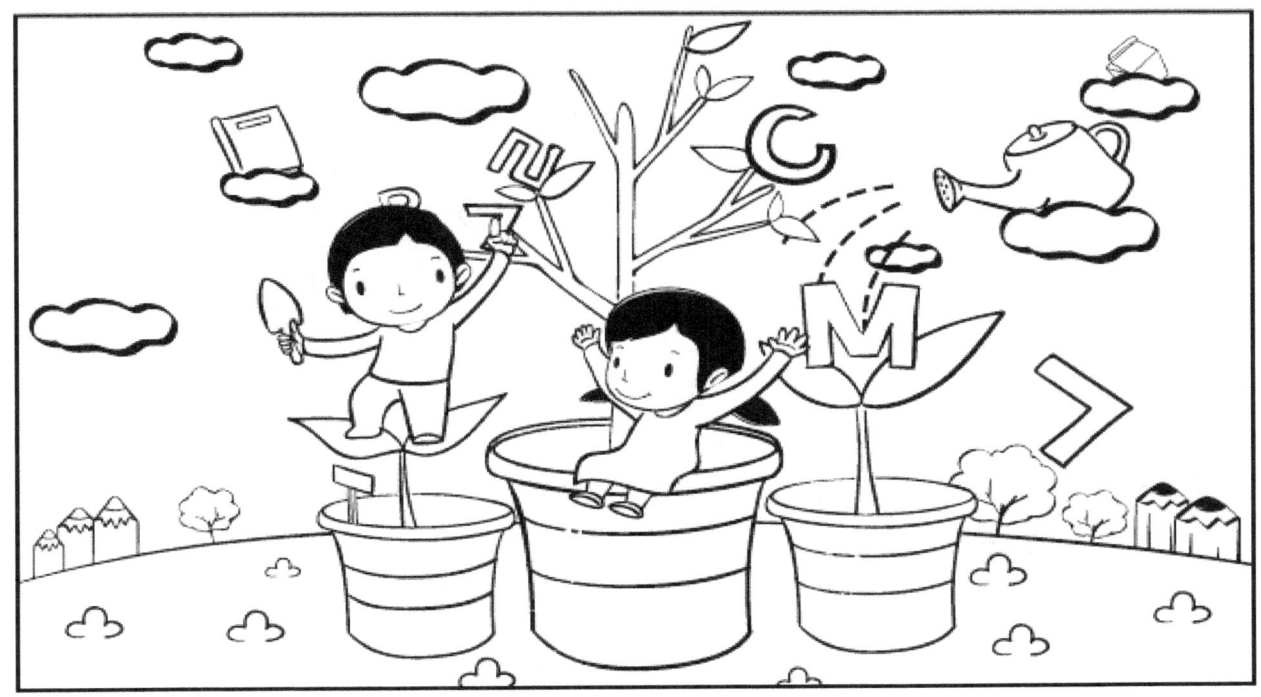

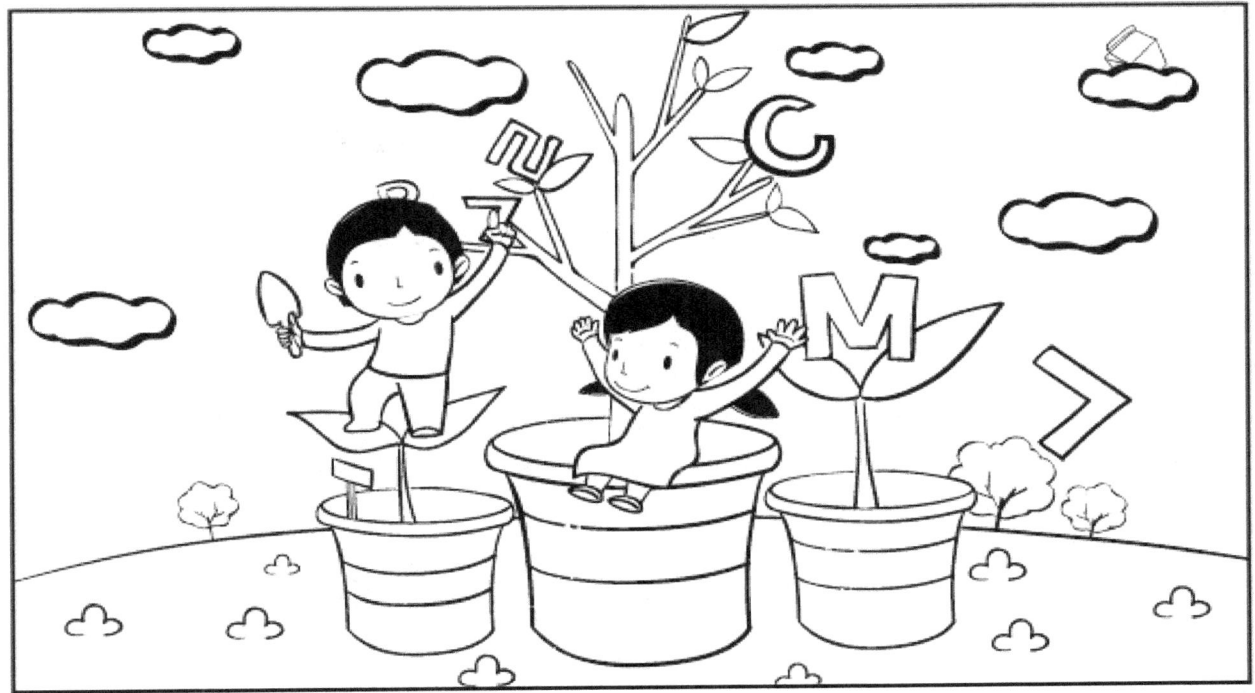

Spot the Differences

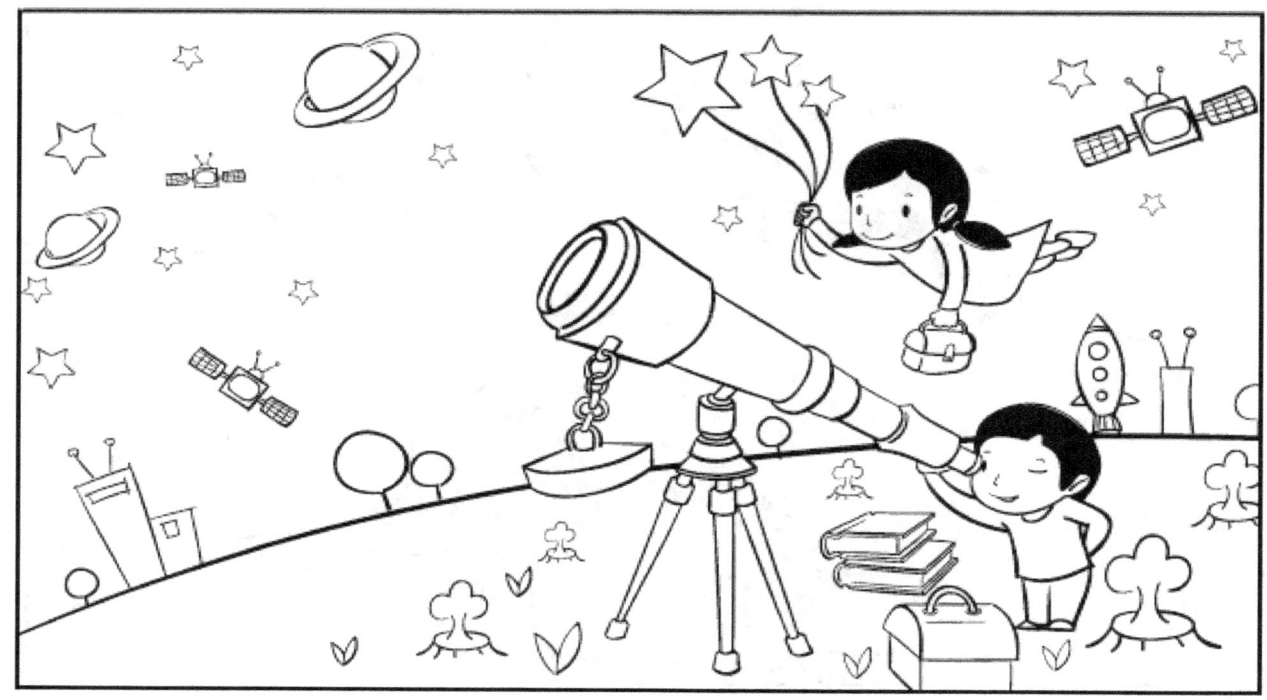

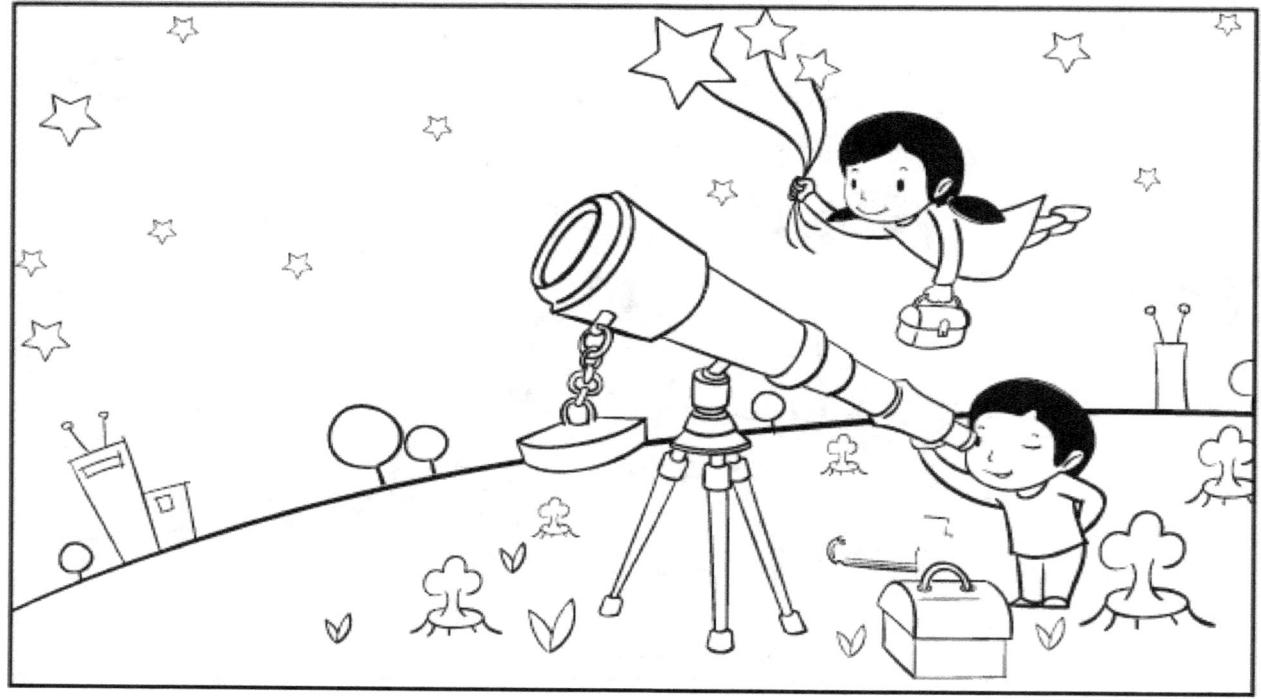

Spot the Differences 33

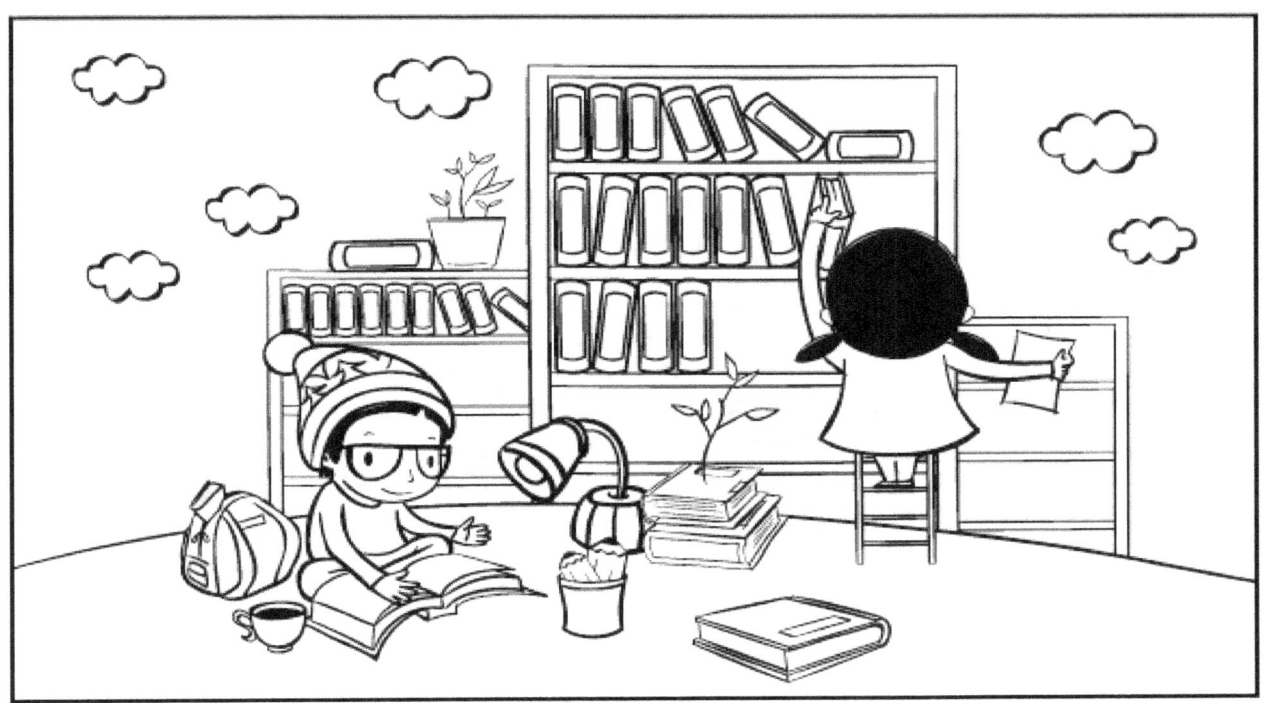

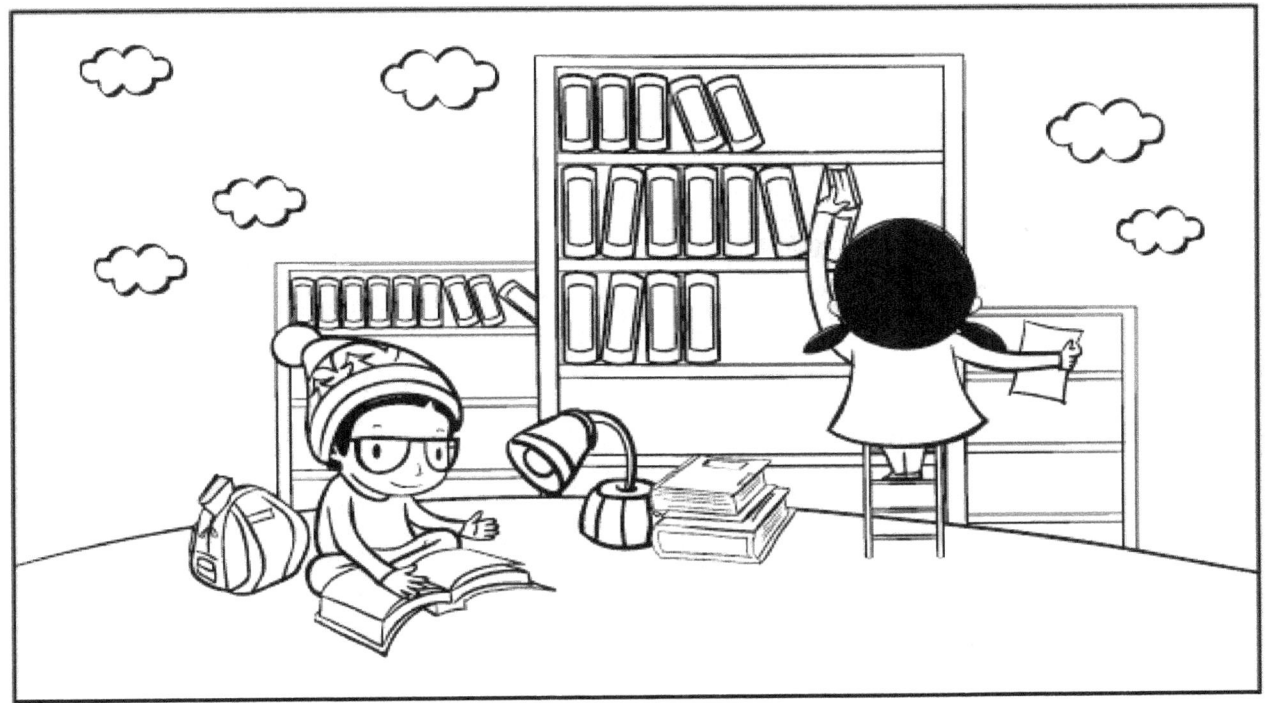

Spot the Differences

34

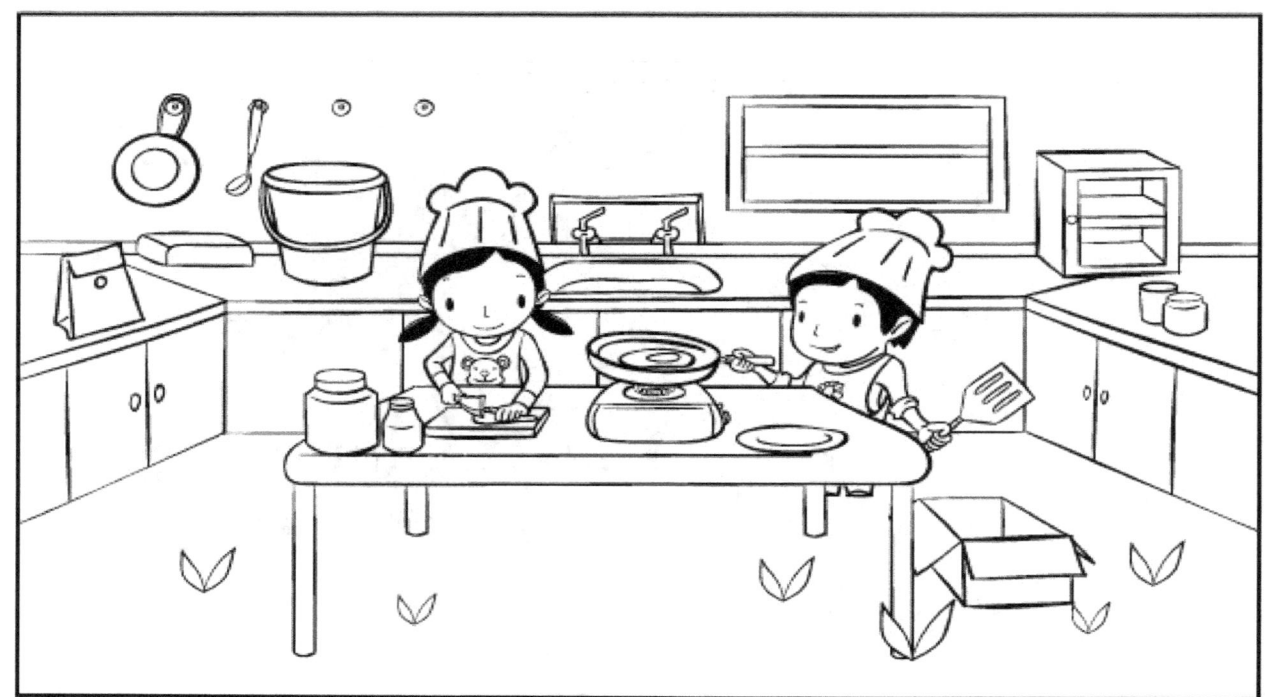

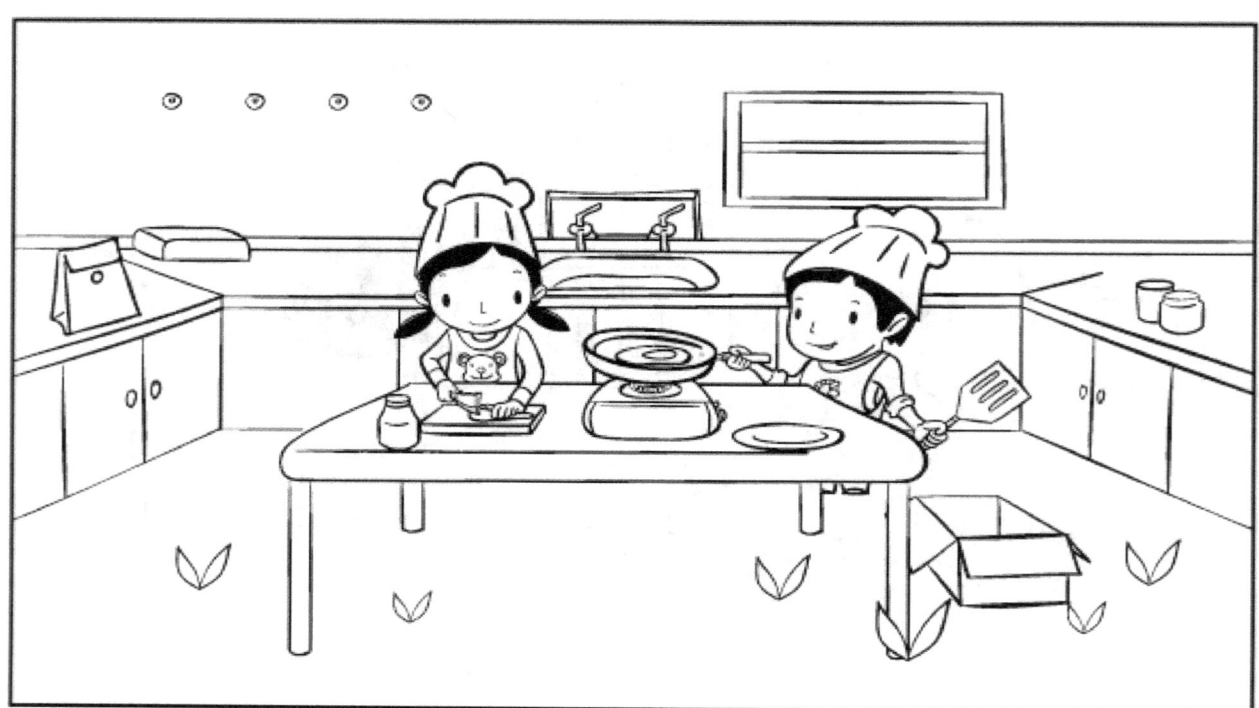

Spot the Differences

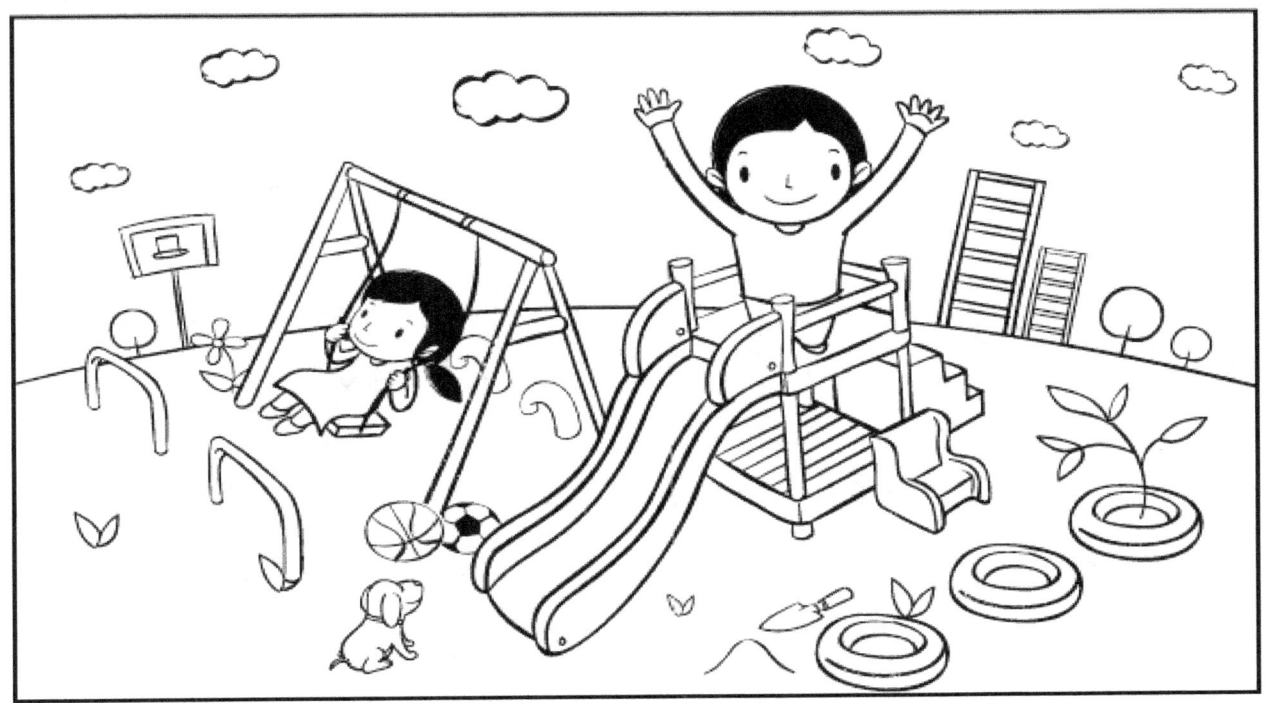

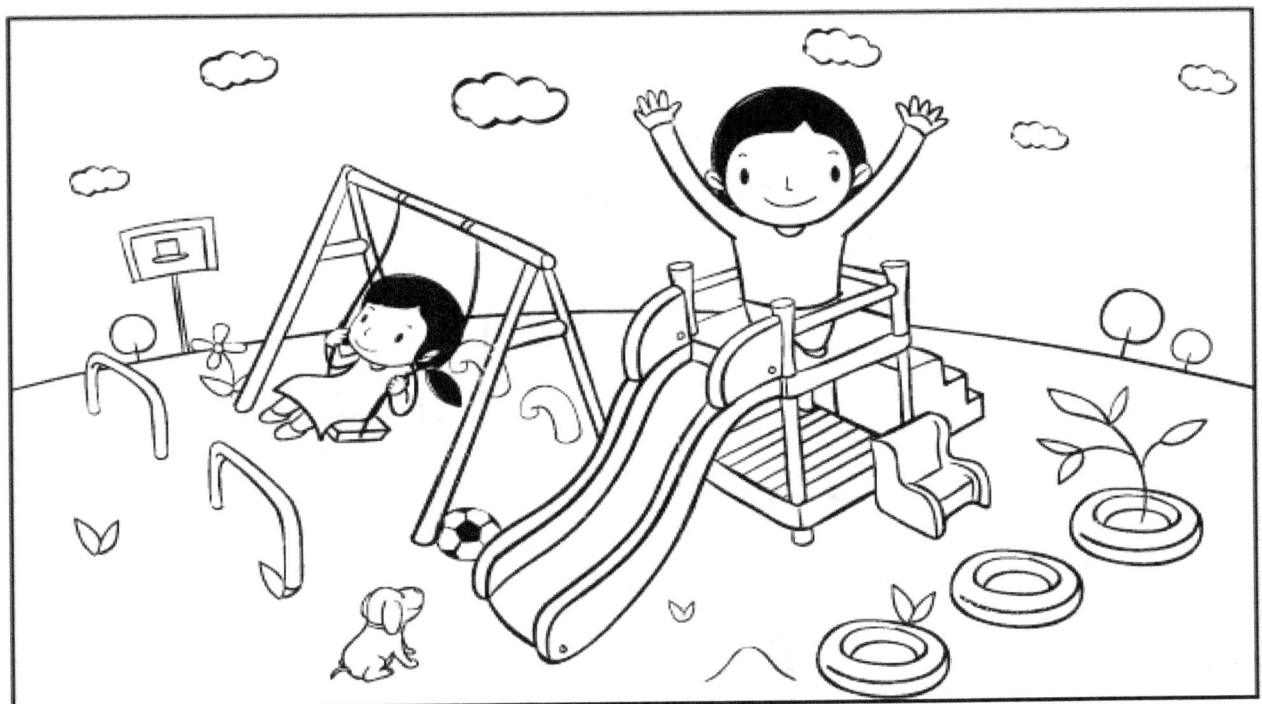

Spot the Differences

36

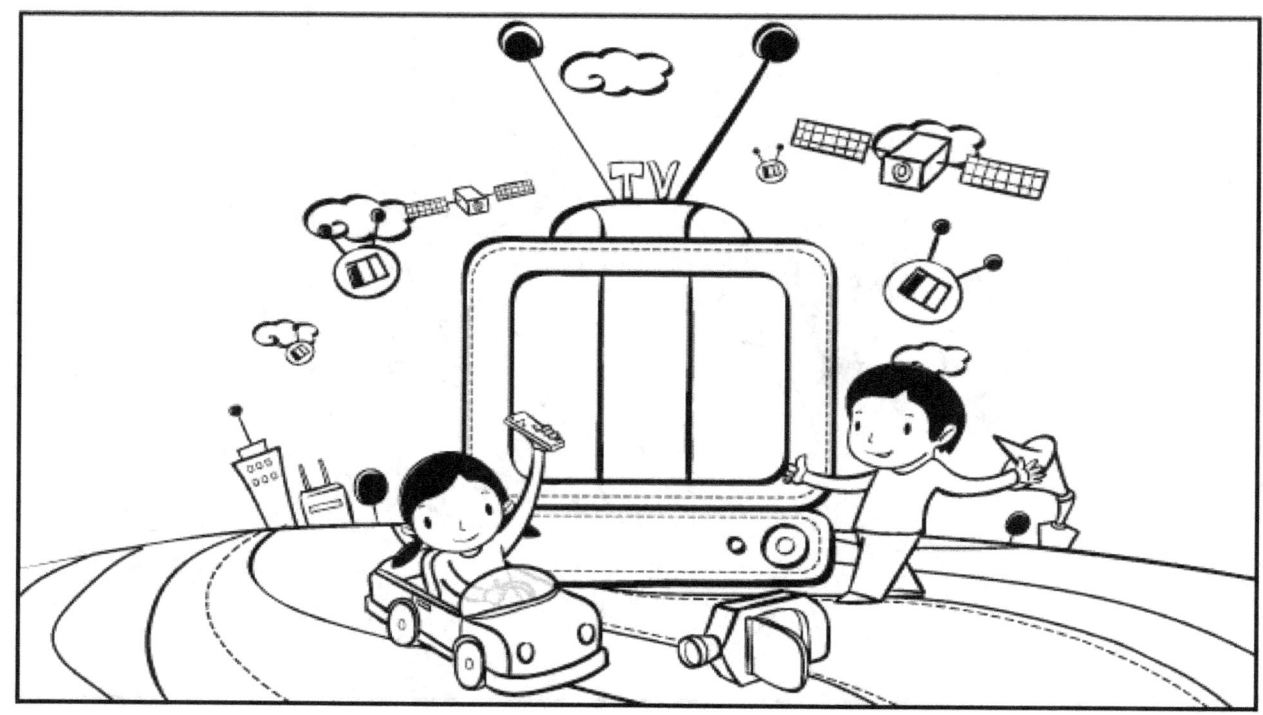

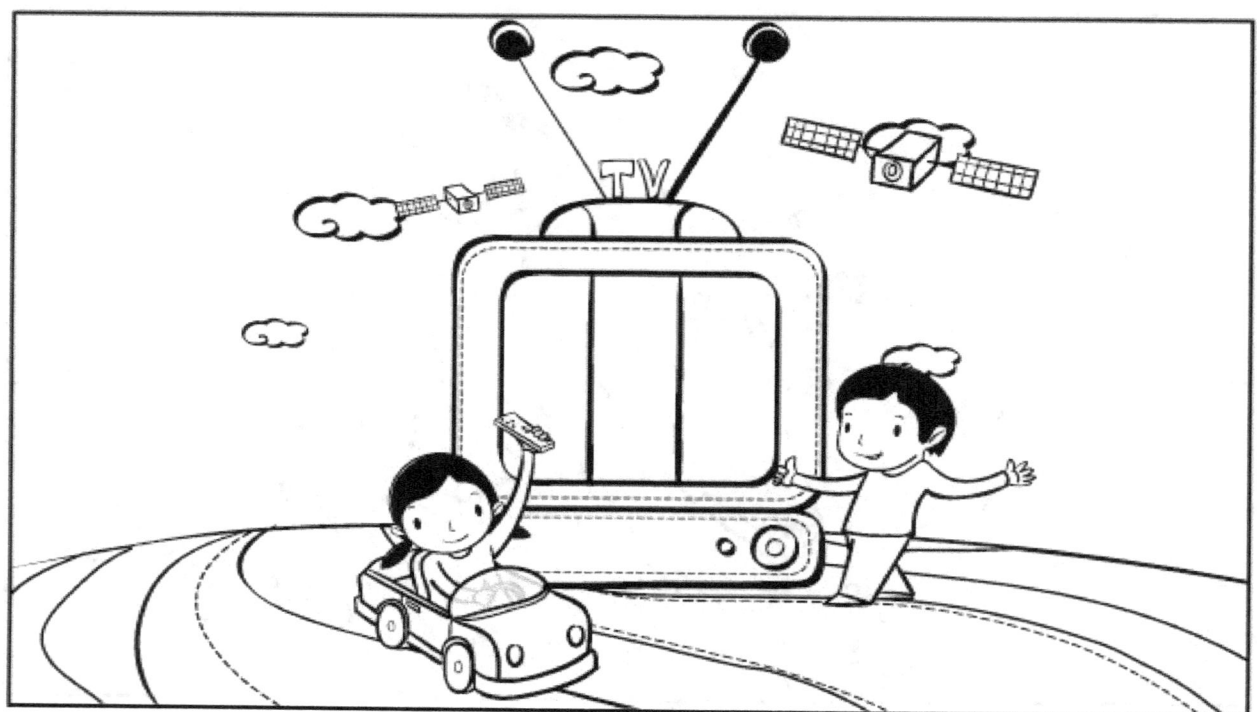

Spot the Differences

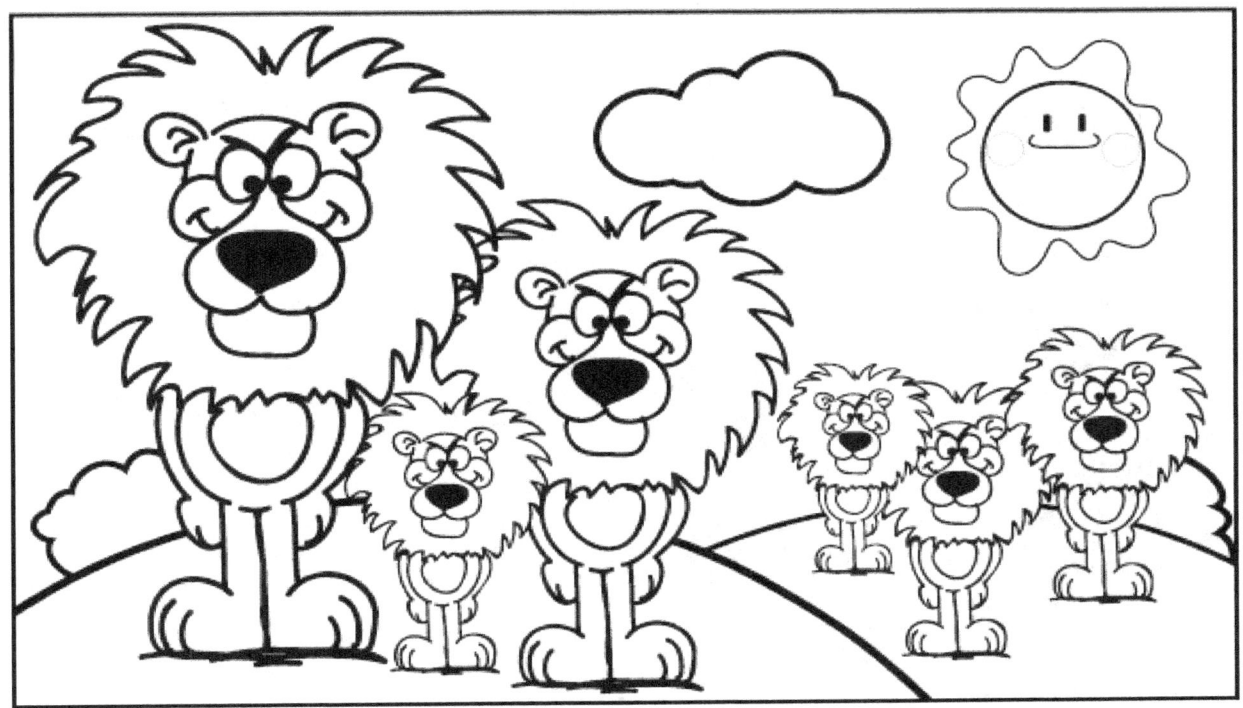

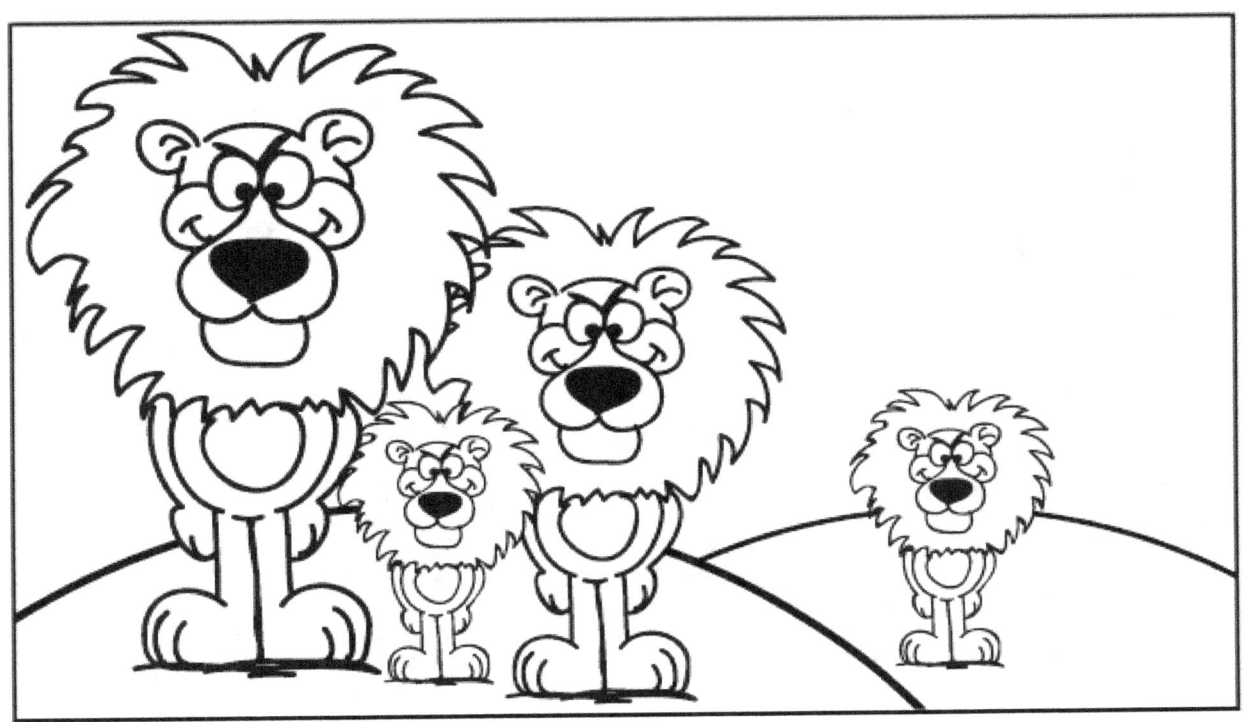

Spot the Differences

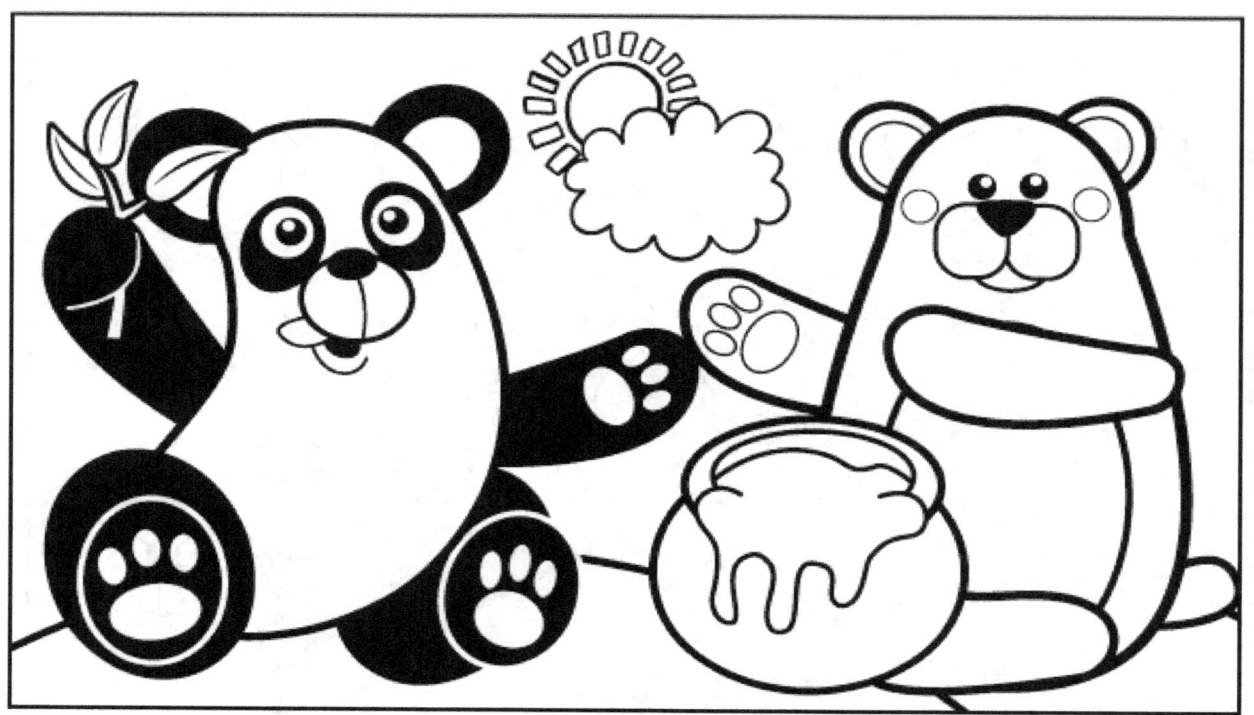

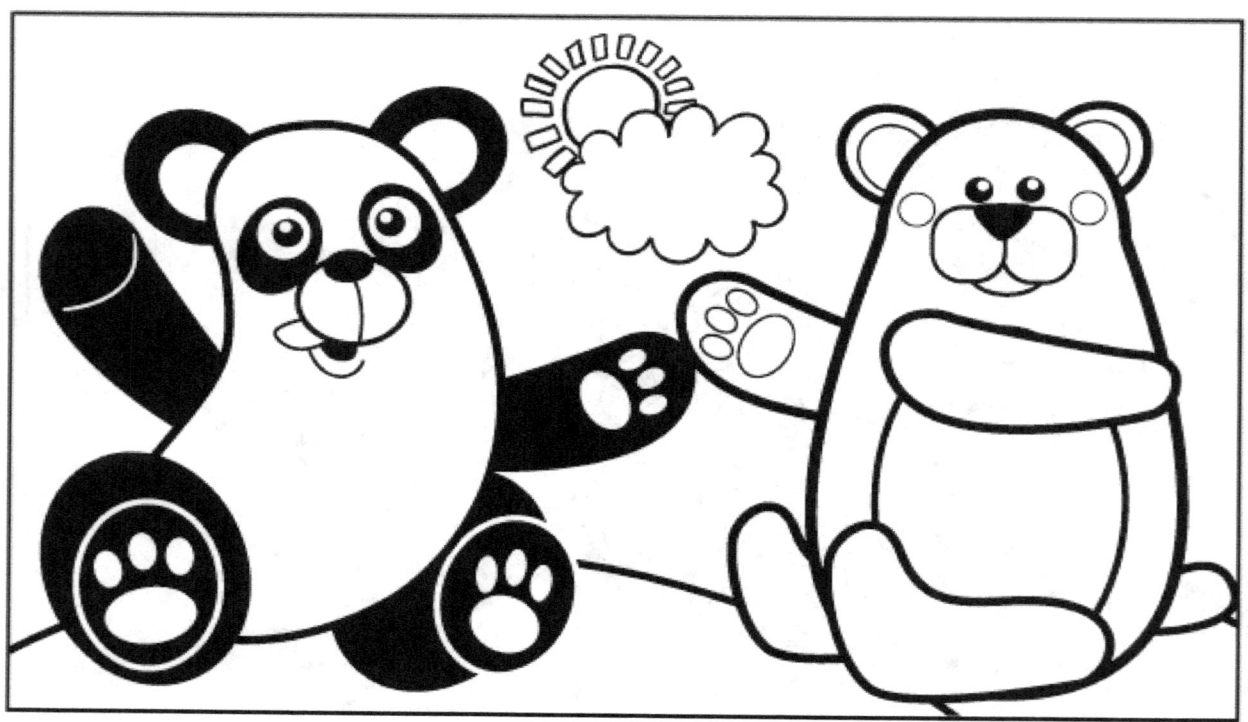

Spot the Differences

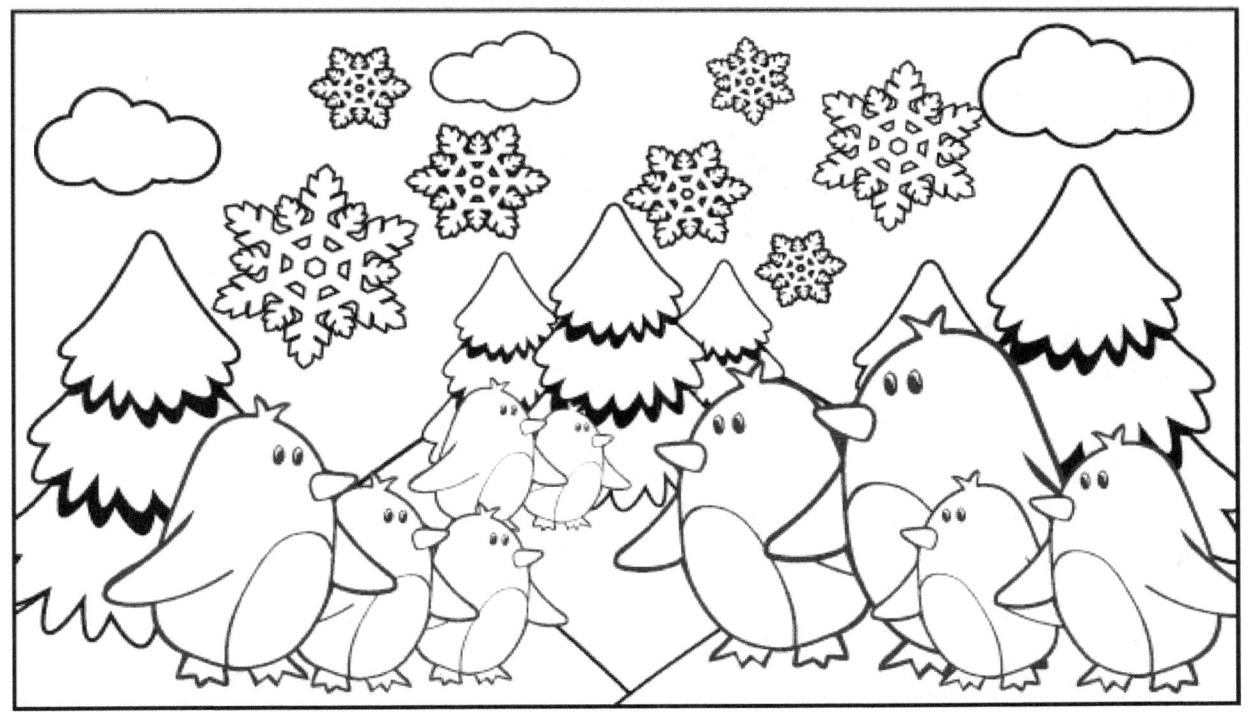

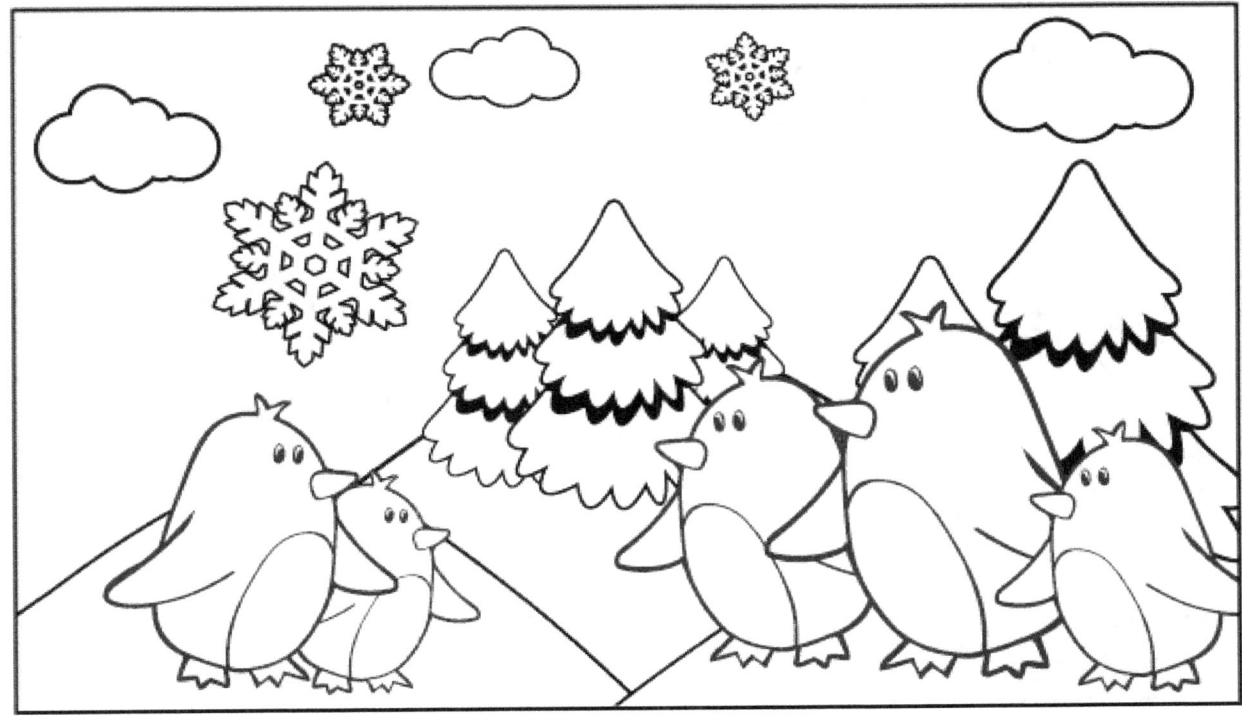

Spot the Differences 40

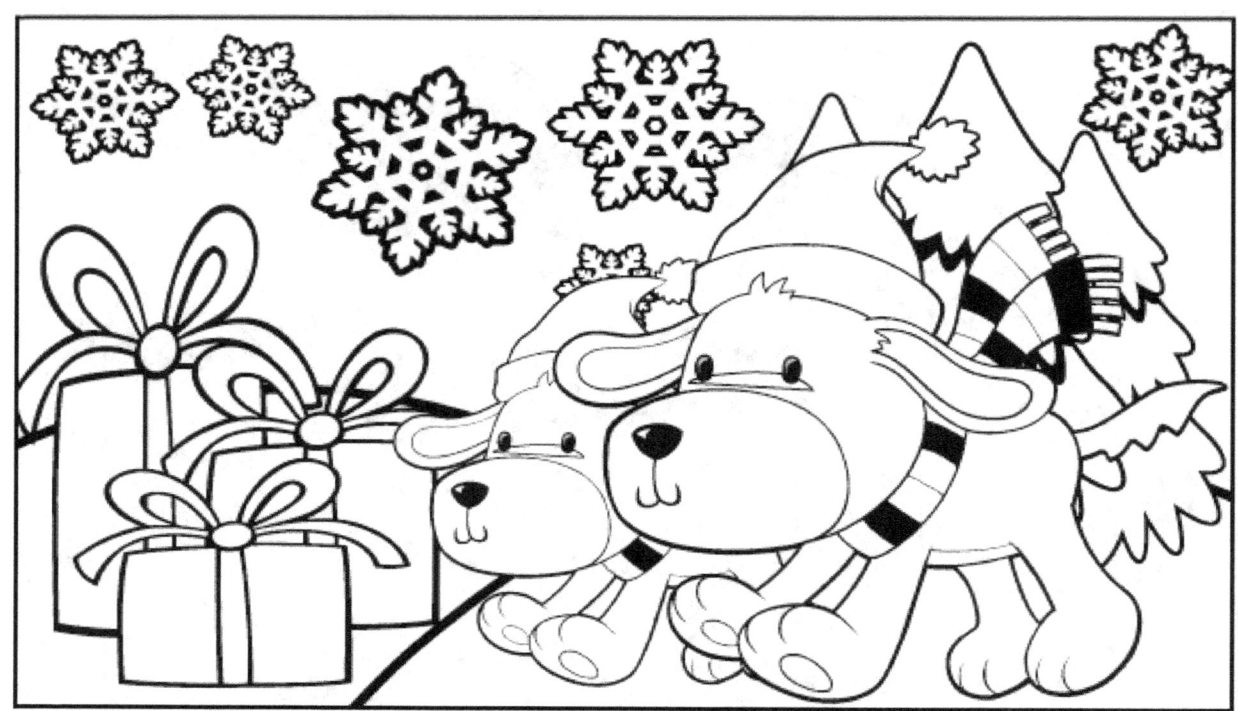

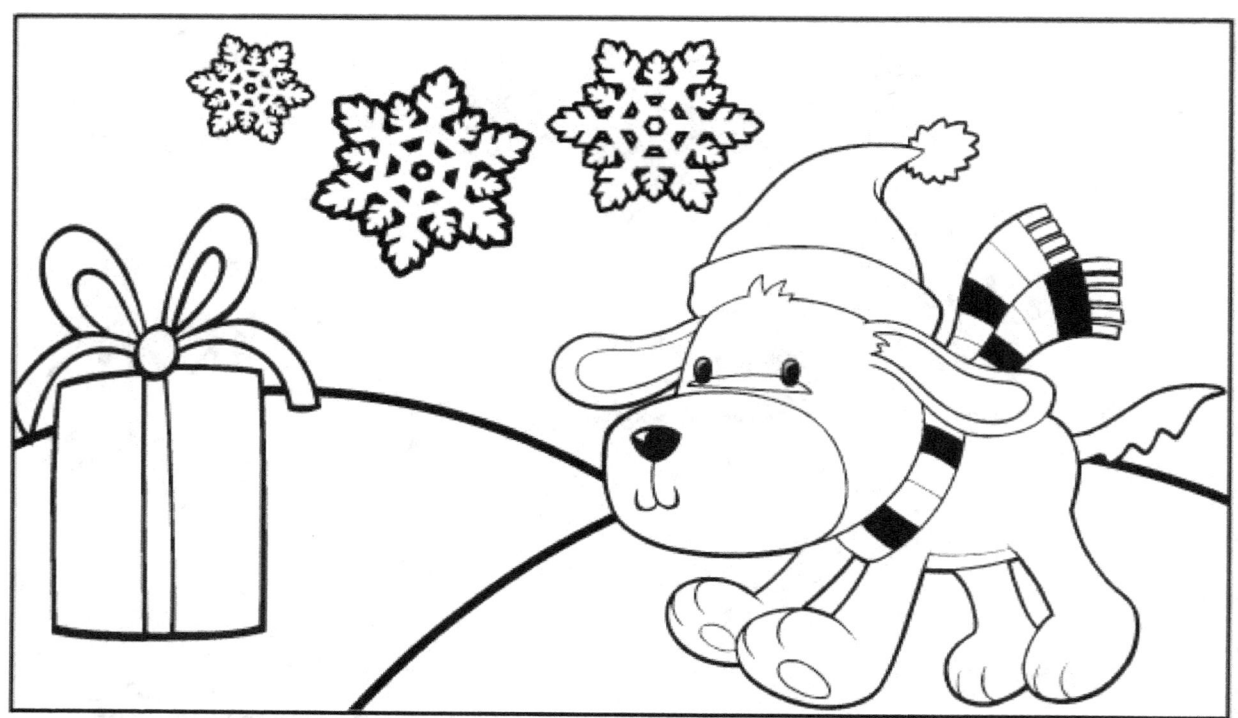

Spot the Differences 41

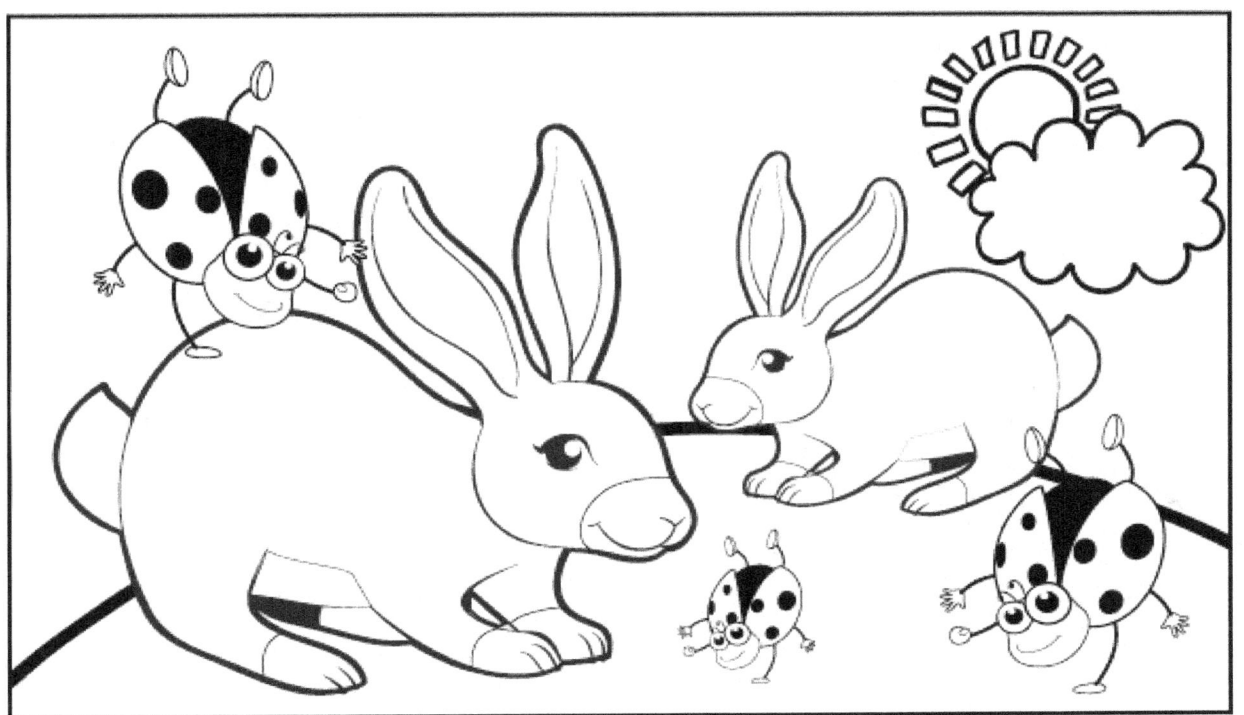

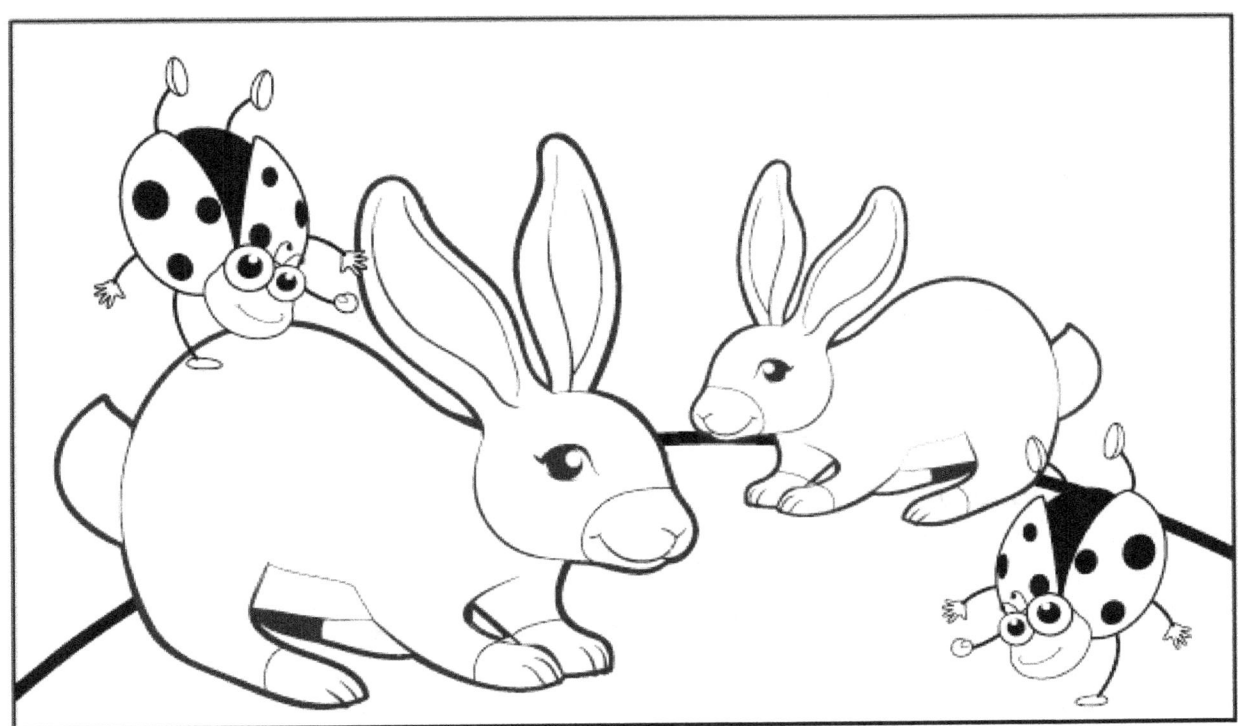

Spot the Differences

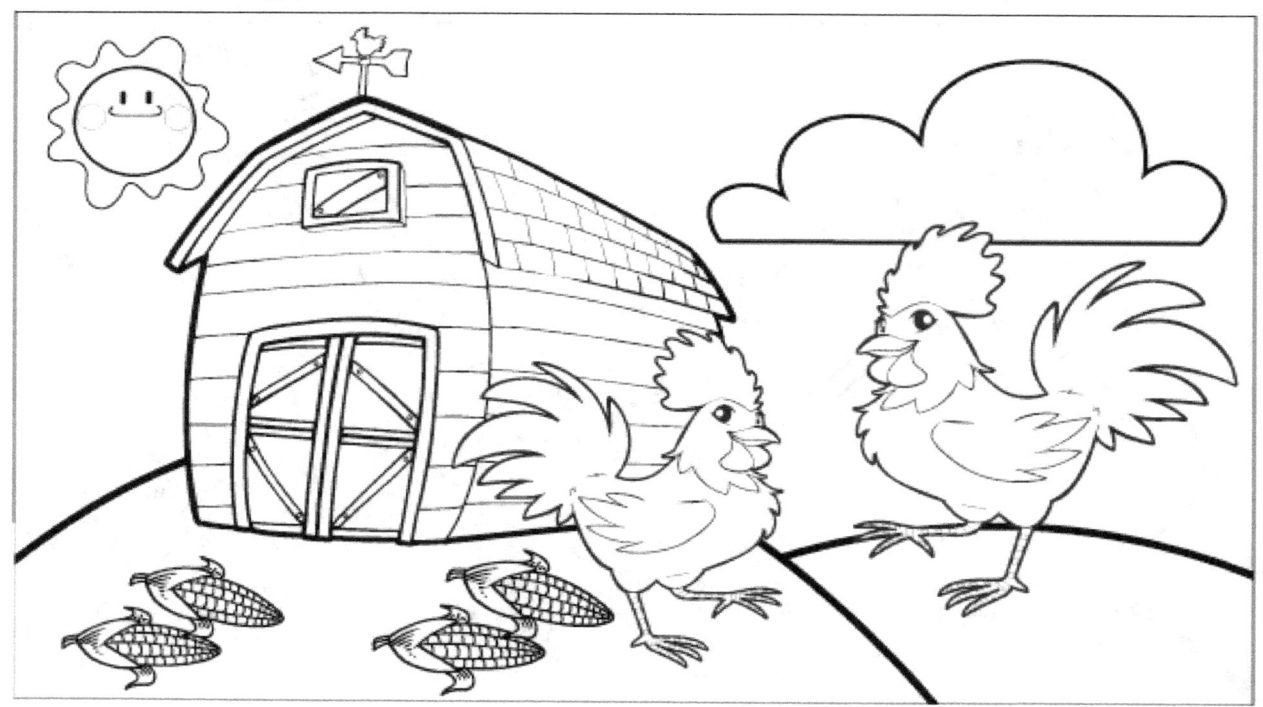

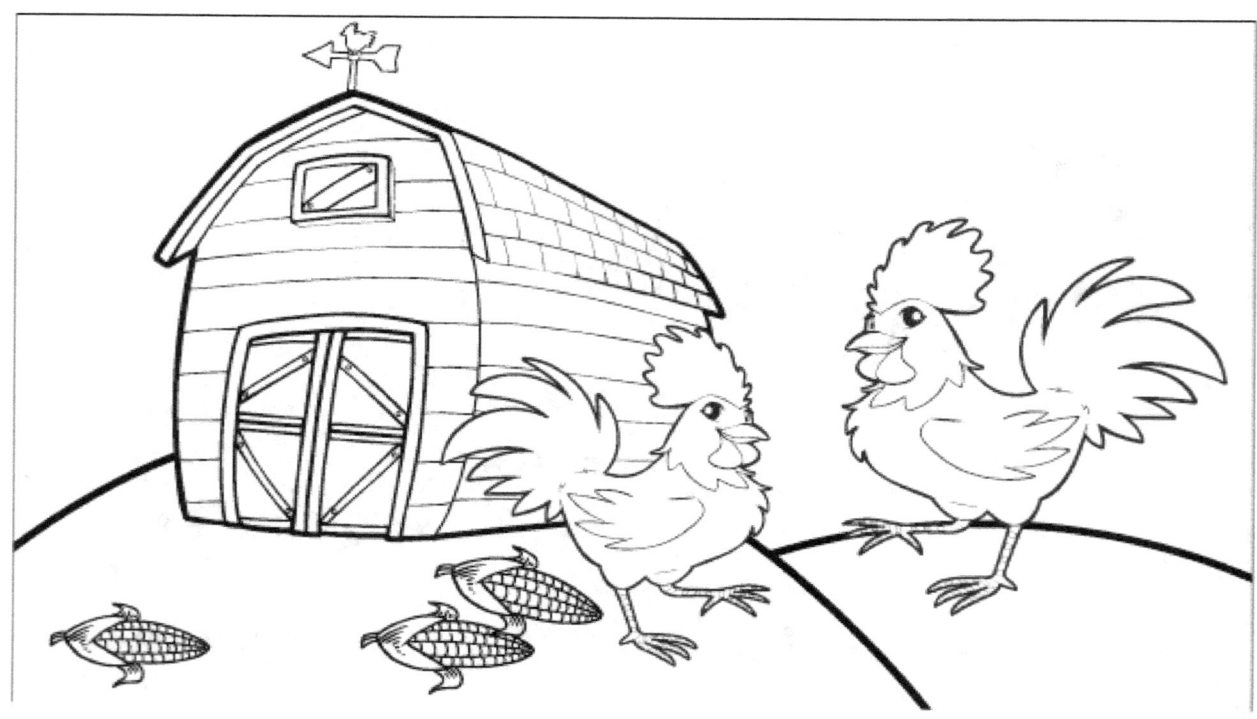

Spot the Differences 43

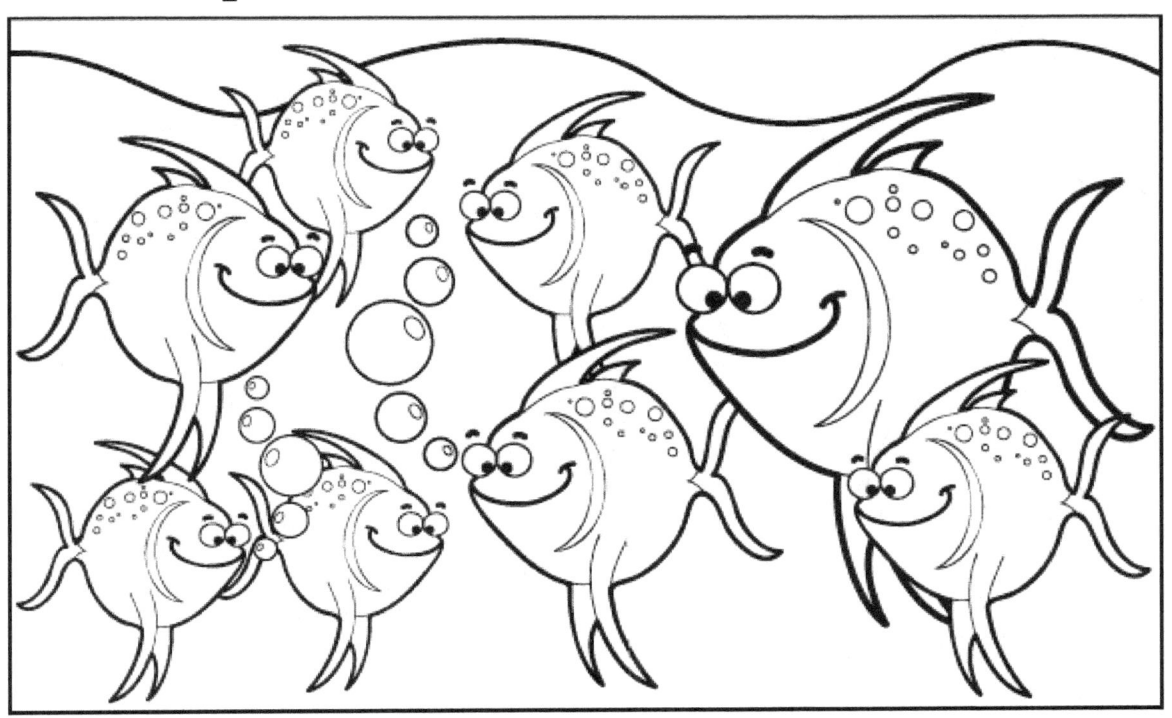

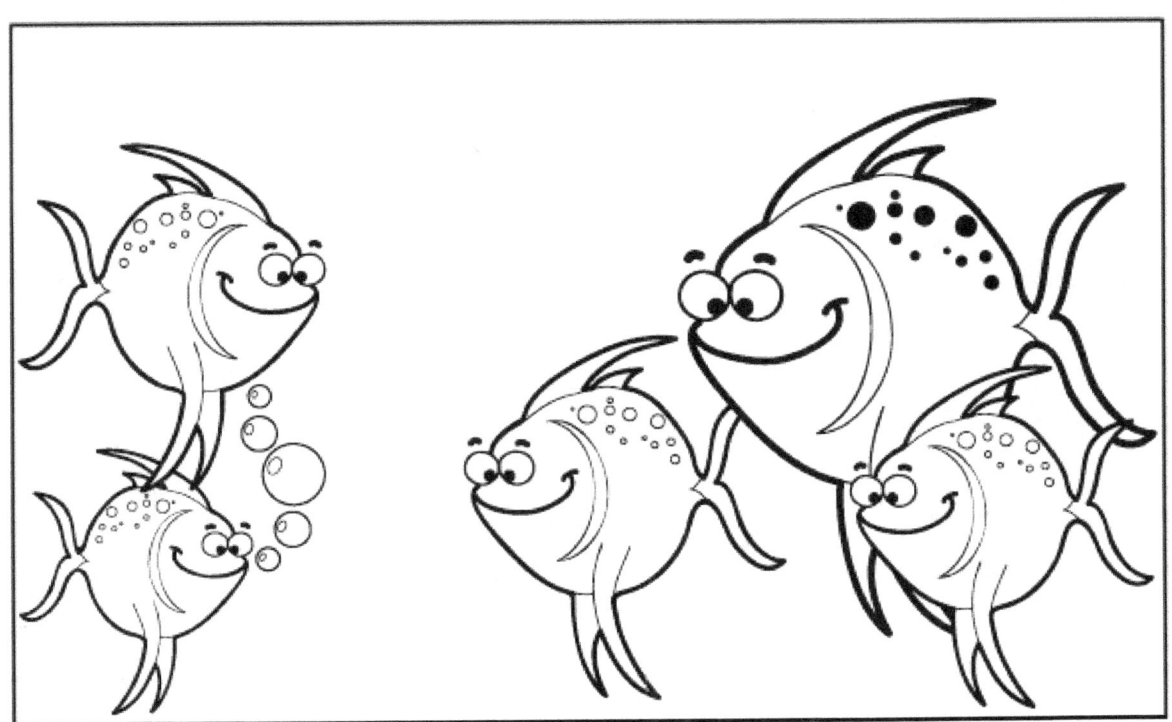

Spot the Differences

44

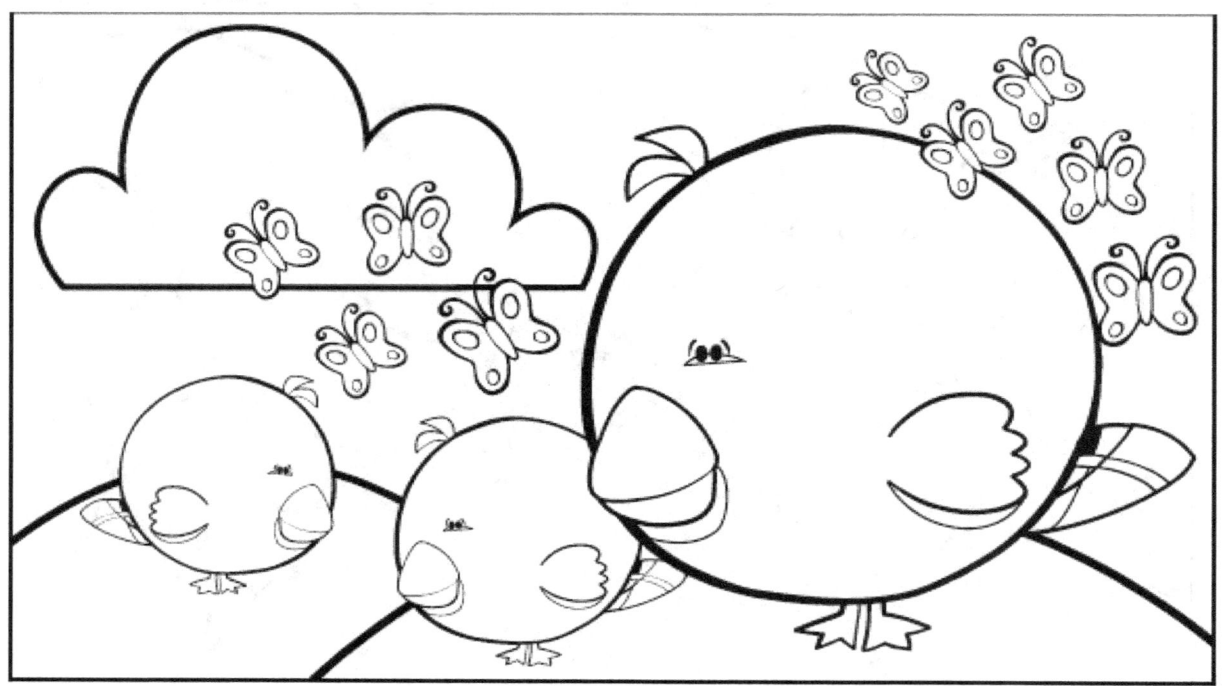

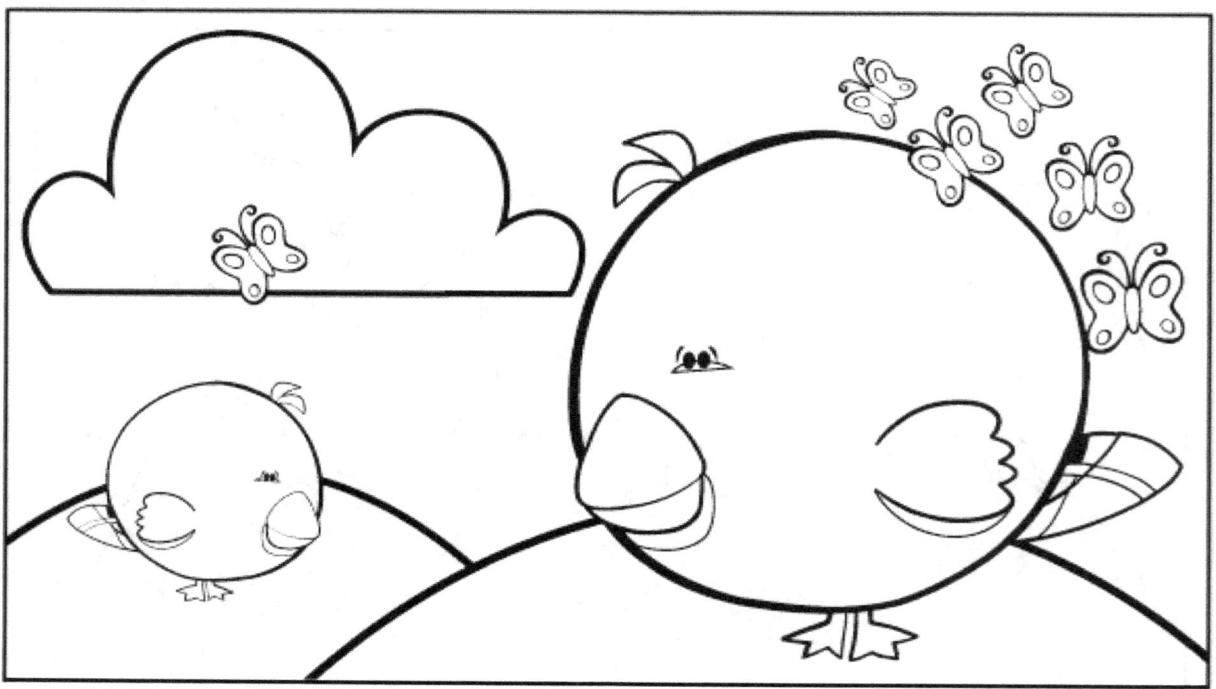

Spot the Differences

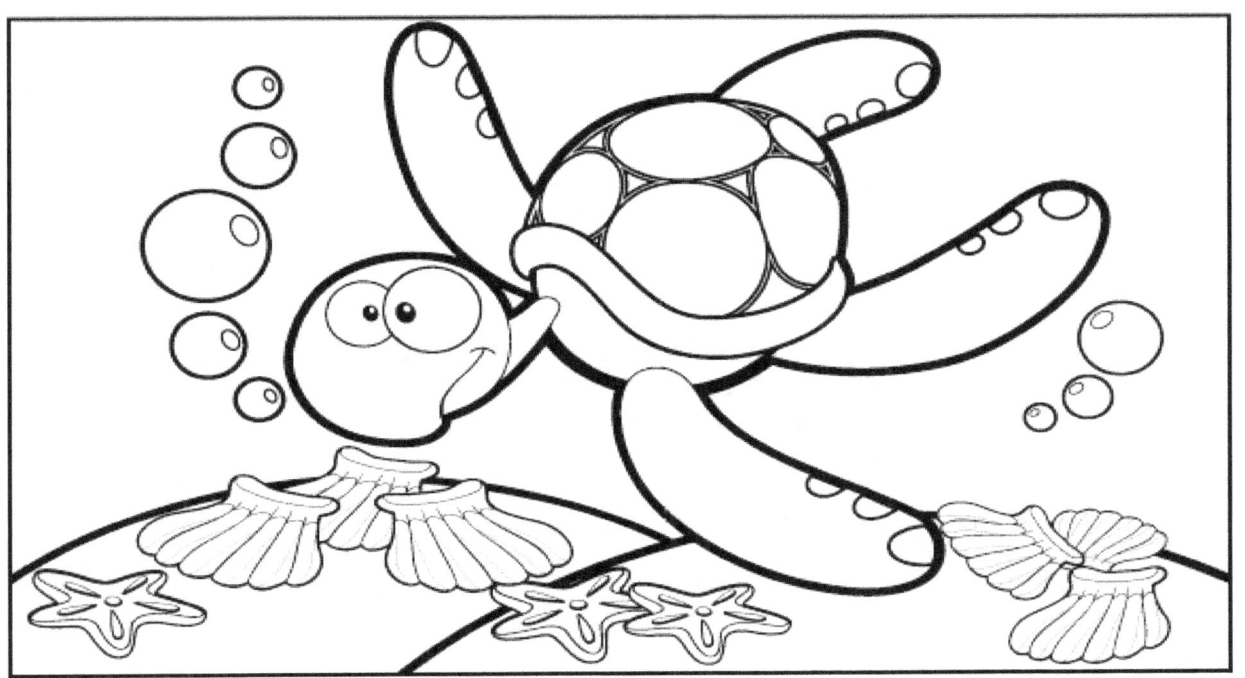

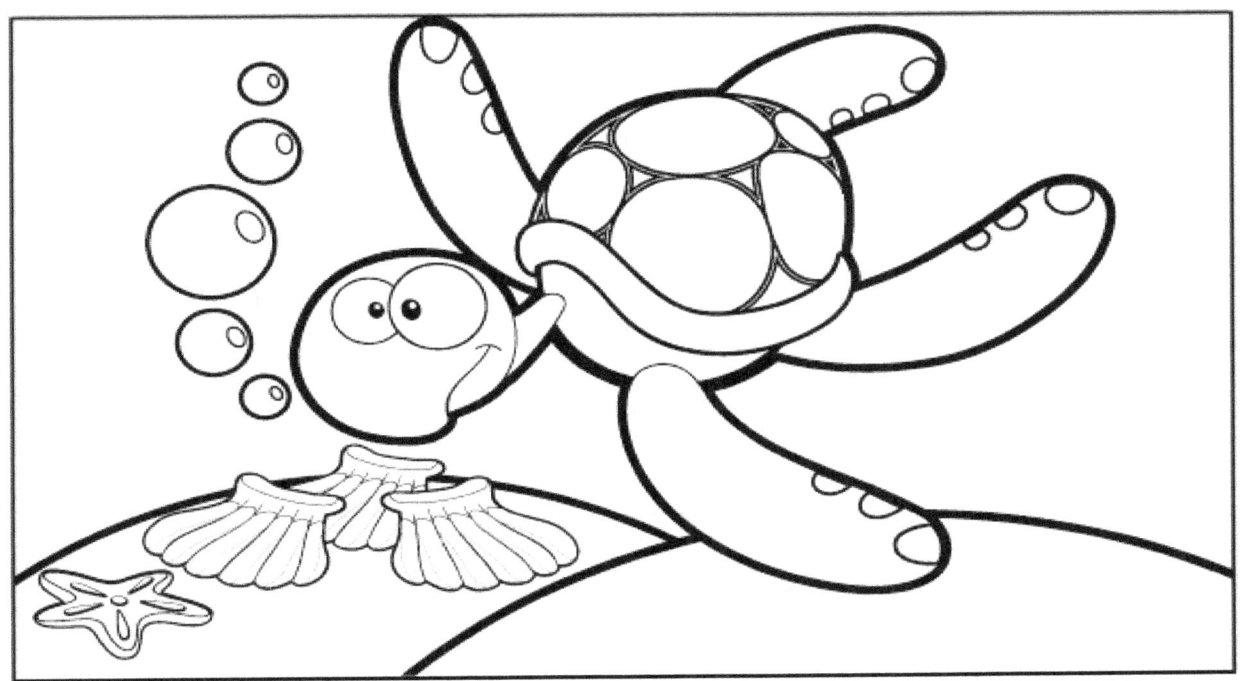

SUDOKU PUZZLE 4x4

A fun activity to reinforce your children's math skills and logical thinking. These **Sudoku Puzzles comes in two levels of difficulty - Beginner and Easy.**

INSTRUCTIONS FOR PLAYING SUDOKU

Each puzzle consists of a 4x4 grid containing given numbers in various places. The object is to fill all empty squares so that the numbers 1 to 4 appear exactly once in each row, column and box.

Here is a blank **4x4 Sudoku Grid** that could be useful in the method of solving the 4x4 Sudoku Puzzles.

46

Puzzle 43
4x4 Easy

			3
	2	1	
	4		
2			1

Puzzle 44
4x4 Easy

	2		3
4			
		3	
	4		1

Puzzle 45
4x4 Easy

	1	4	
			2
1			
	3	2	

Puzzle 46
4x4 Easy

4			
	2	4	
3			1
		3	

Puzzle 47
4x4 Easy

			4
4		3	
2		1	
	1		

Puzzle 48
4x4 Easy

			1
	4	3	
	2		
4			3

Puzzle 49
4x4 Easy

		3	
	2		1
2		1	
	4		

Puzzle 50
4x4 Easy

	4		1
2			
	2		3
		1	

Puzzle 51
4x4 Easy

	3		4
		2	
	1		
3		4	

Puzzle 52
4x4 Easy

4			2
		4	
3			1
	1		

Puzzle 53
4x4 Easy

3		4	
	1		
1		2	
			4

Puzzle 54
4x4 Easy

4		1	
	2		
			1
2		3	

Puzzle 55
4x4 Easy

	1			2
			4	
	3			4
		1		

Puzzle 56
4x4 Easy

			1
1		4	
2		3	
	3		

Puzzle 57
4x4 Easy

	2		
4			2
3			1
		3	

Puzzle 58
4x4 Easy

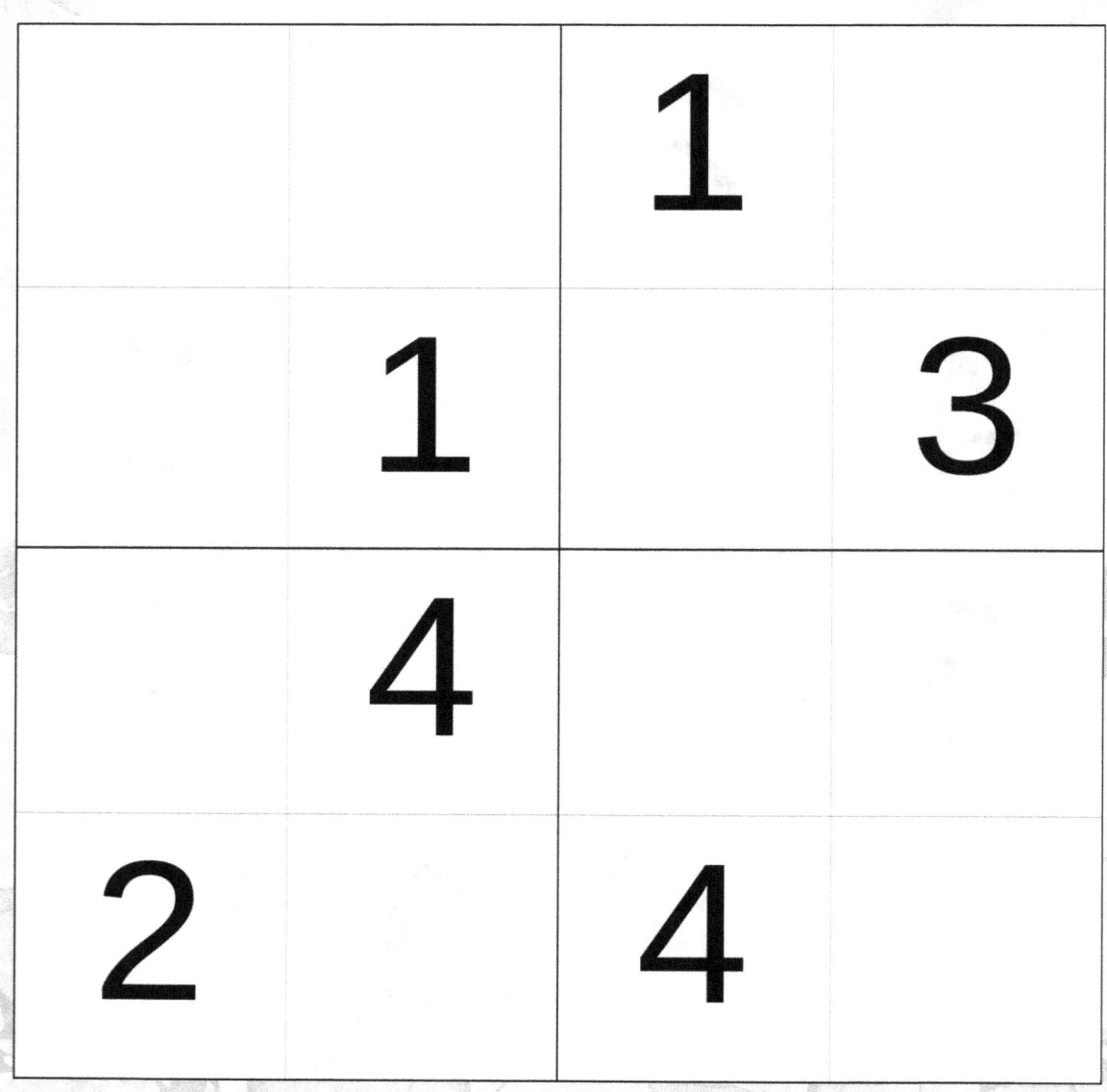

Puzzle 59
4x4 Easy

		4	
4			2
1			
	3	1	

Puzzle 60
4x4 Easy

	1		2
		4	
	3		4
1			

Puzzle 61
4x4 Easy

	2	1	
4			
2			1
		3	

Puzzle 62
4x4 Easy

	2		
4		2	
1		3	
			1

Cat Shaped Word Search

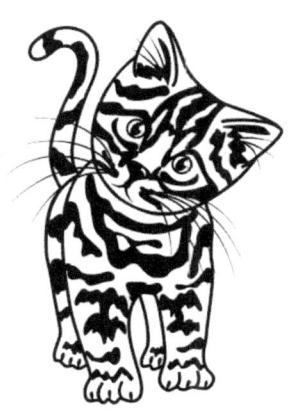

Purr-fect puzzle to excite kids, especially if they have a pet cat. It is also a fun activity to help reinforce and improve your child spelling ability as they get familiar with new words and develop problem-solving skills.

INSTRUCTIONS TO PLAY

Find and circle all of the words listed that are hidden in the different grids. The words may be hidden in any direction and can appear straight across, backward, up and down, down and up and diagonally.

Check your work with the answers on the solution pages 91-56

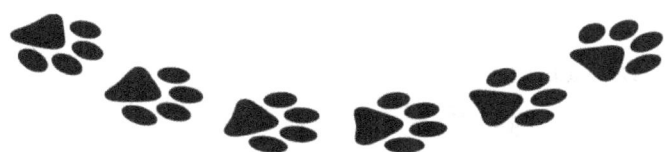

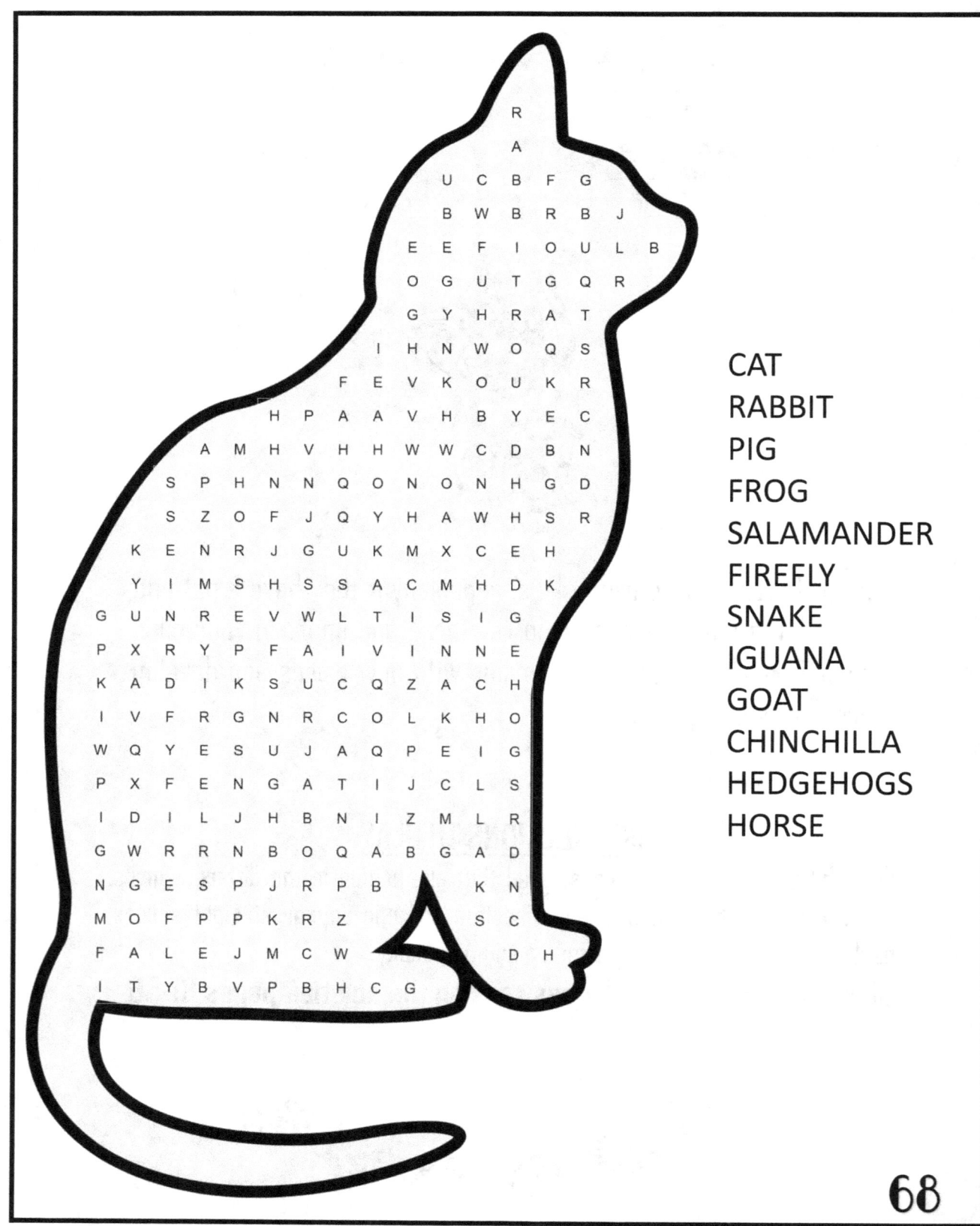

CAT
RABBIT
PIG
FROG
SALAMANDER
FIREFLY
SNAKE
IGUANA
GOAT
CHINCHILLA
HEDGEHOGS
HORSE

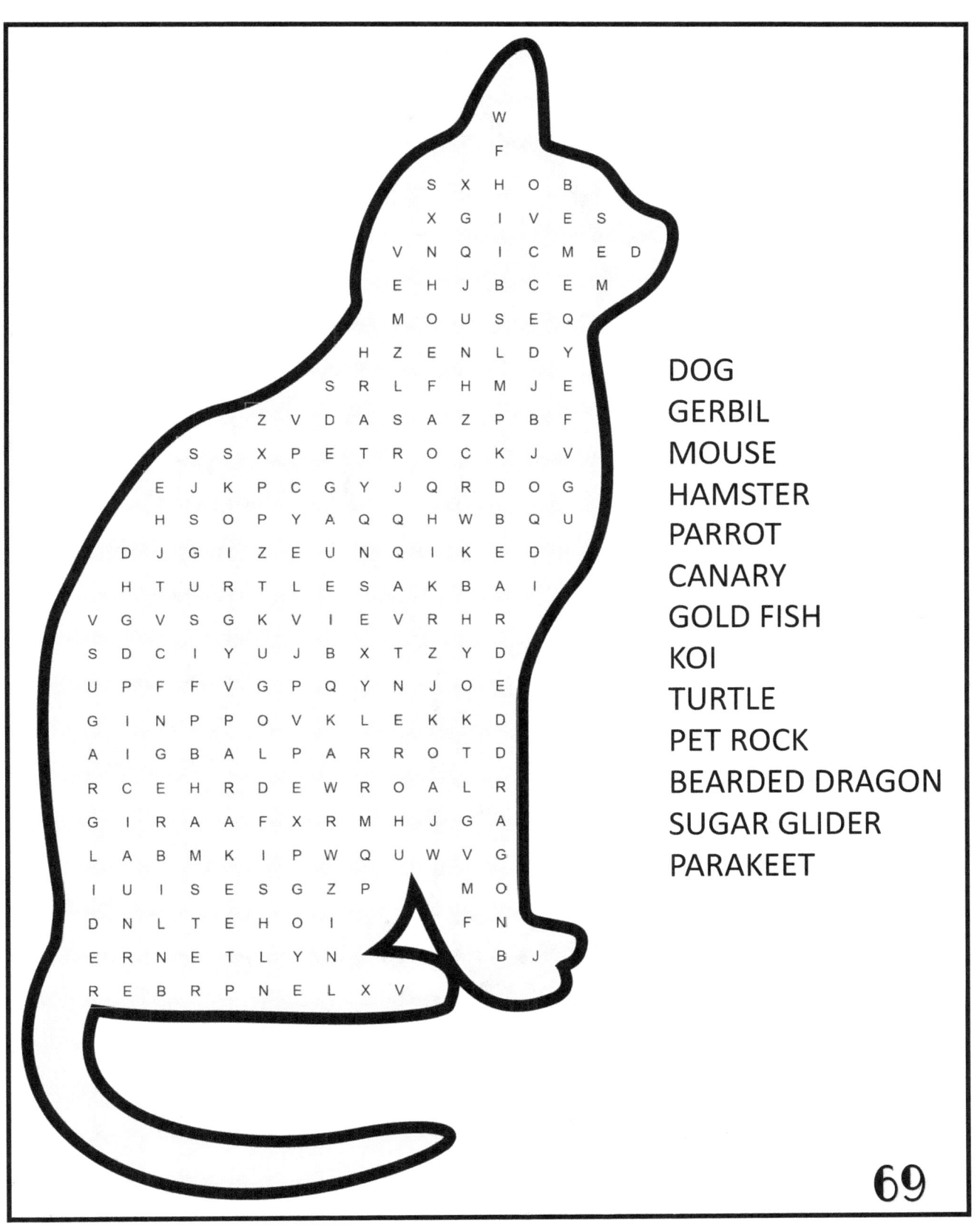

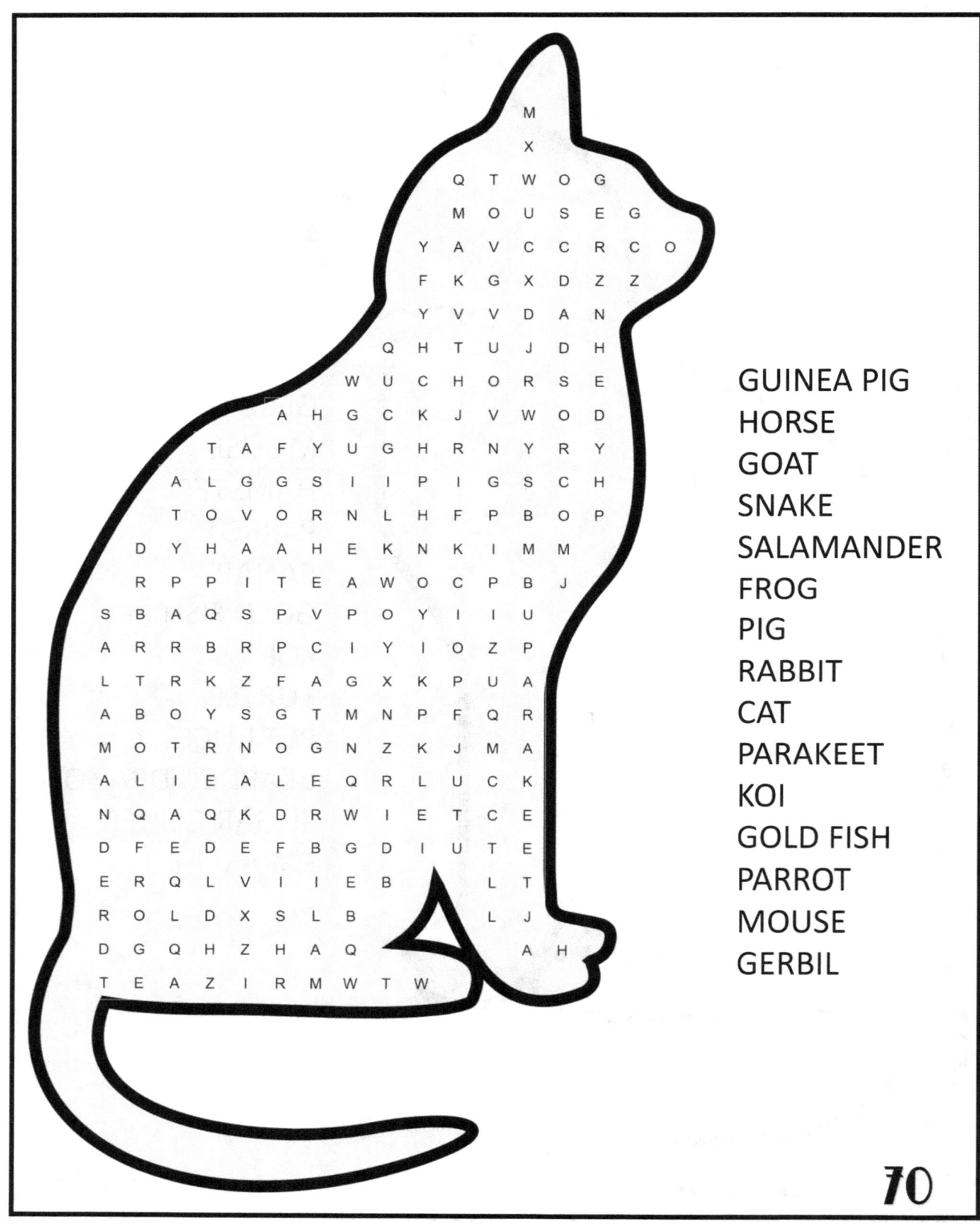

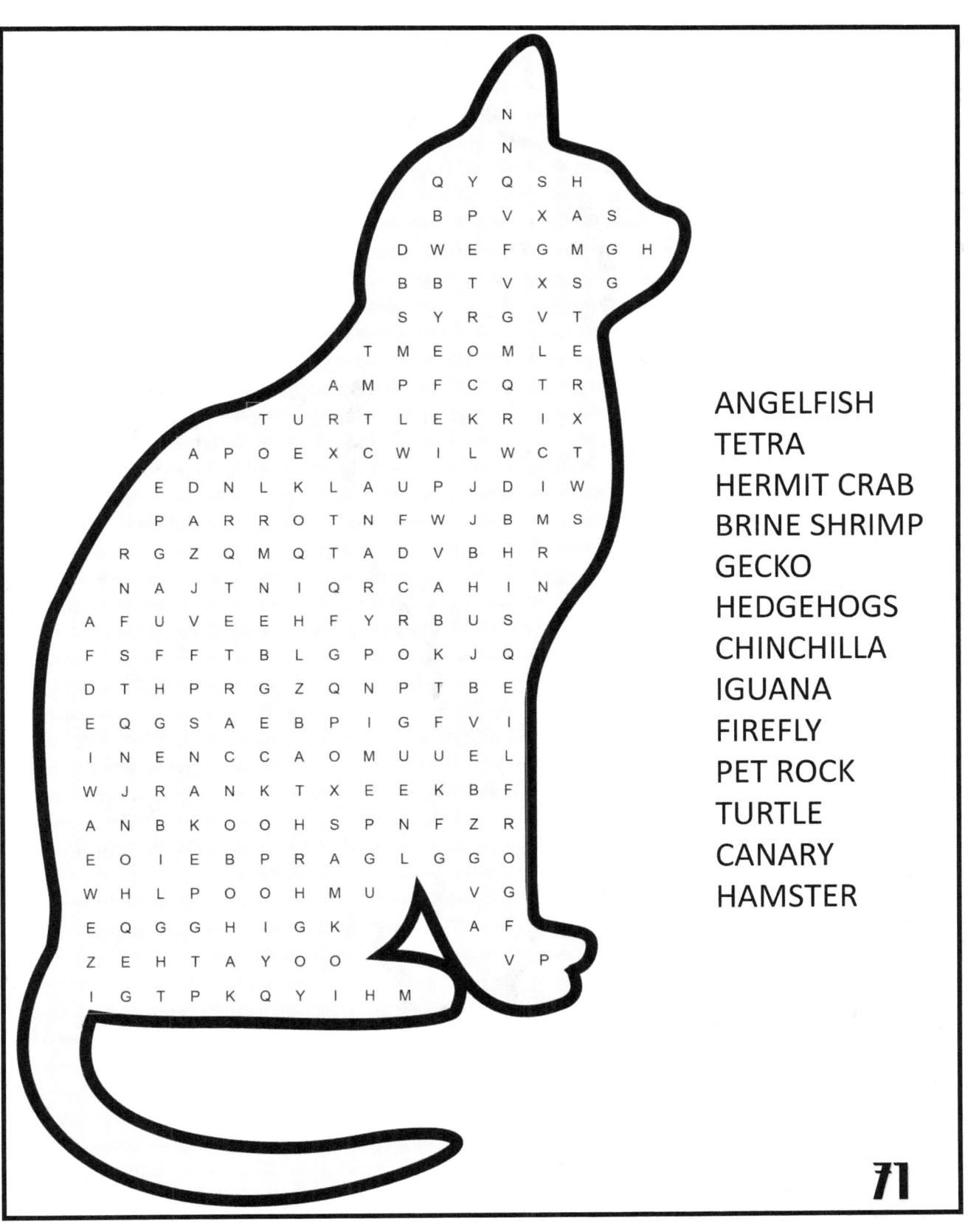

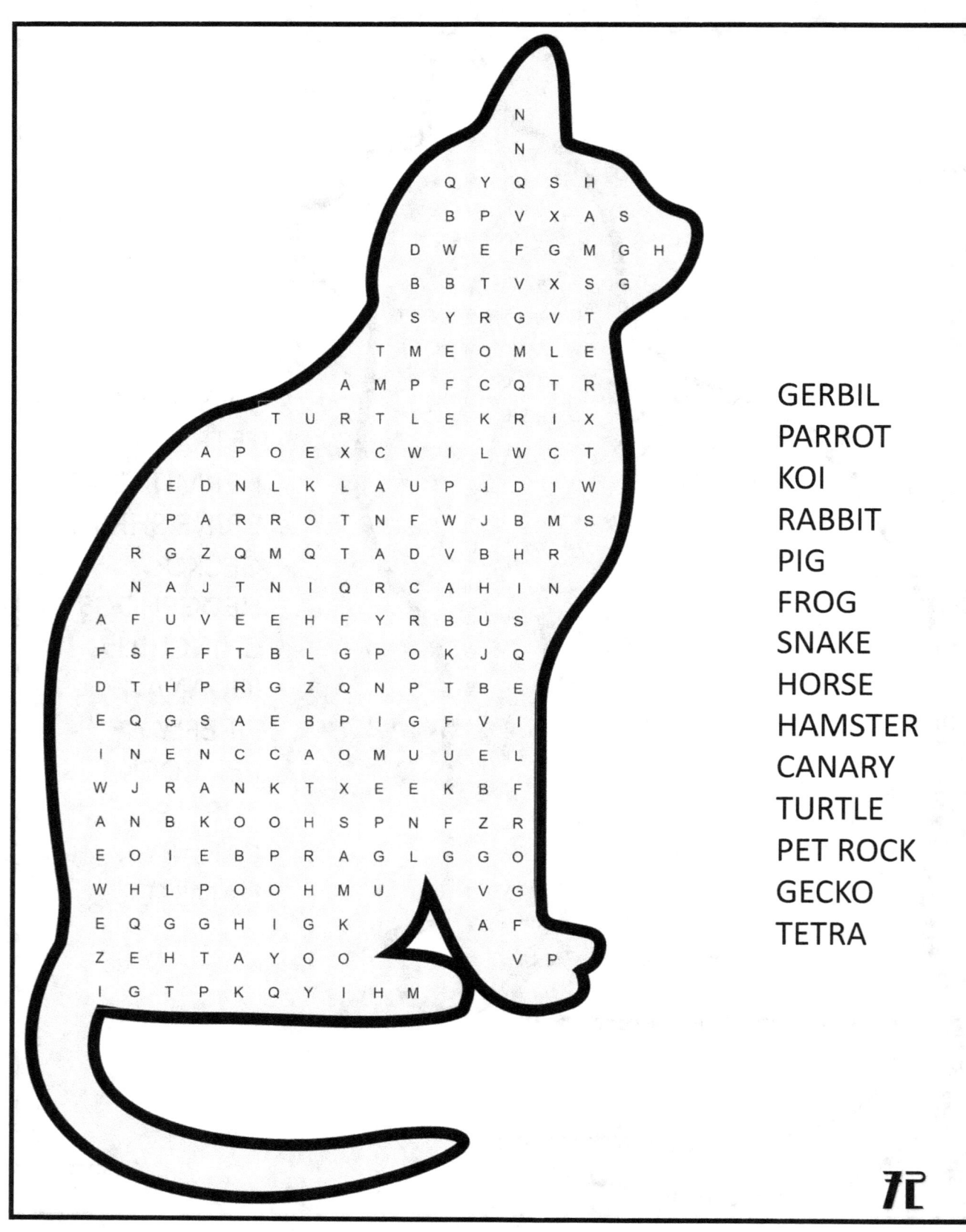

MAZE PUZZLE SOLUTION

Solution for Puzzle 1

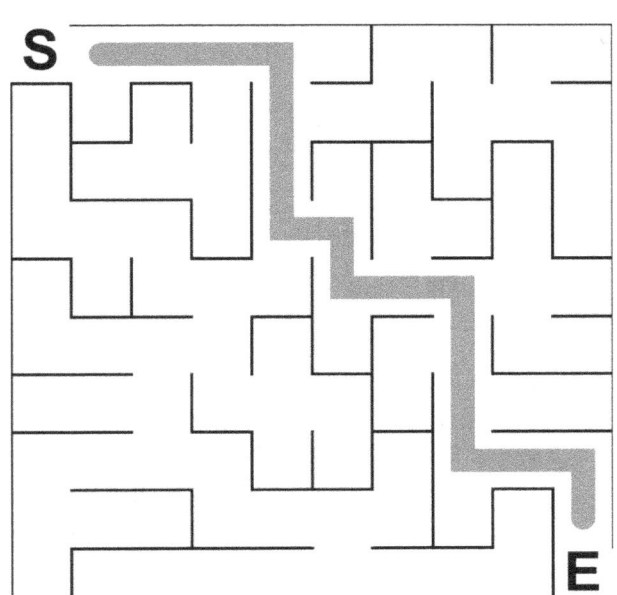

Solution for Puzzle 2

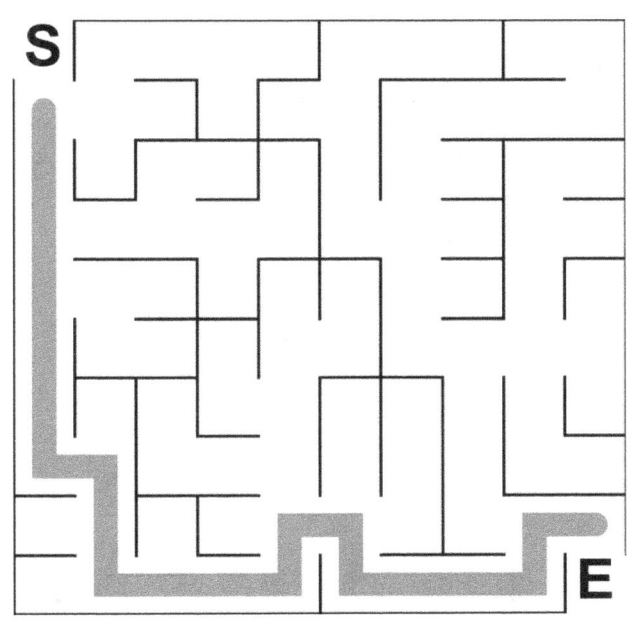

Solution for Puzzle 3

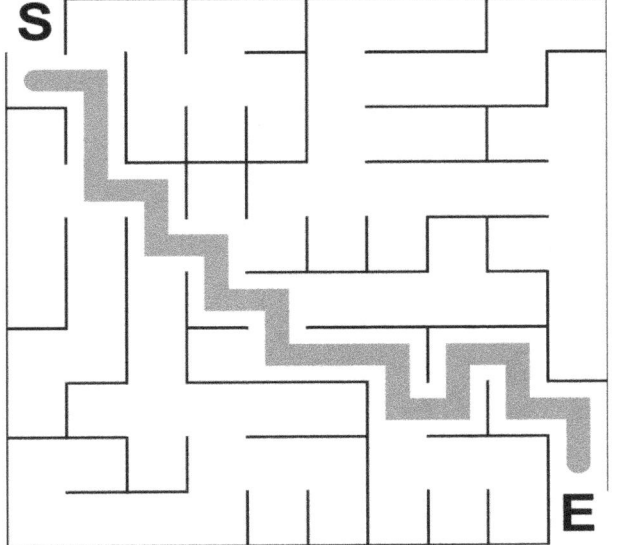

Solution for Puzzle 4

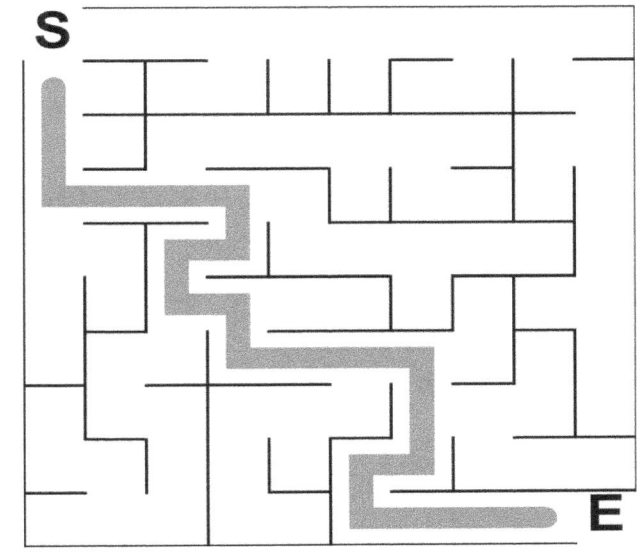

MAZE PUZZLE SOLUTION

Solution for Puzzle 5

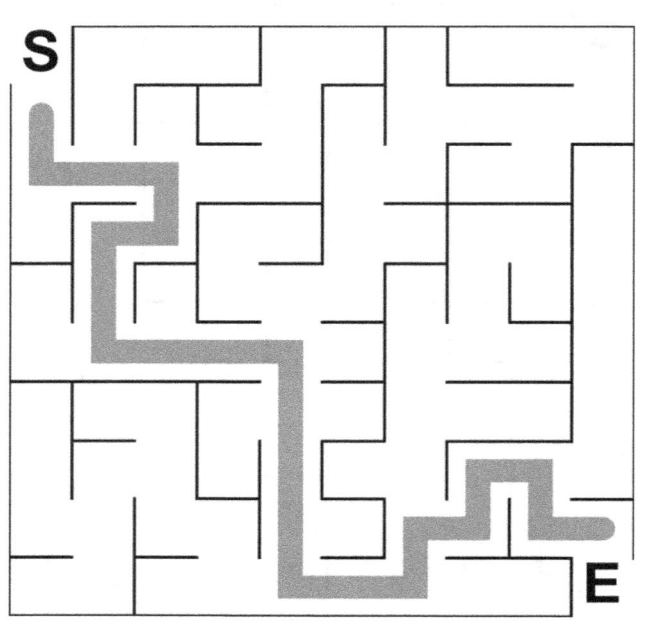

Solution for Puzzle 6

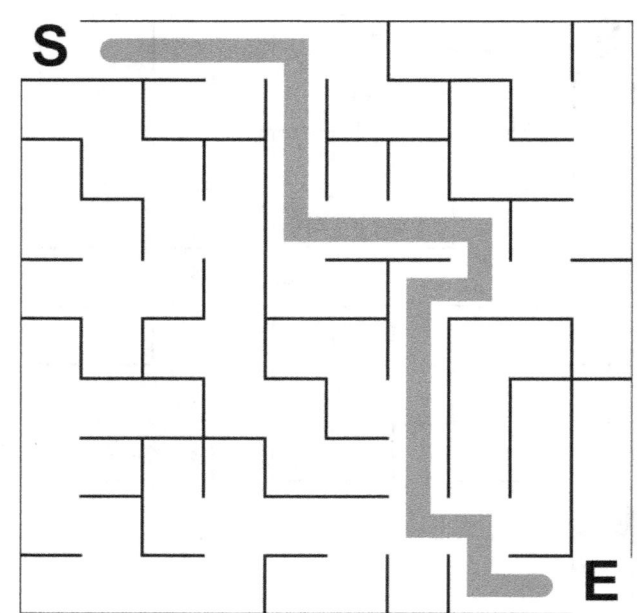

Solution for Puzzle 7

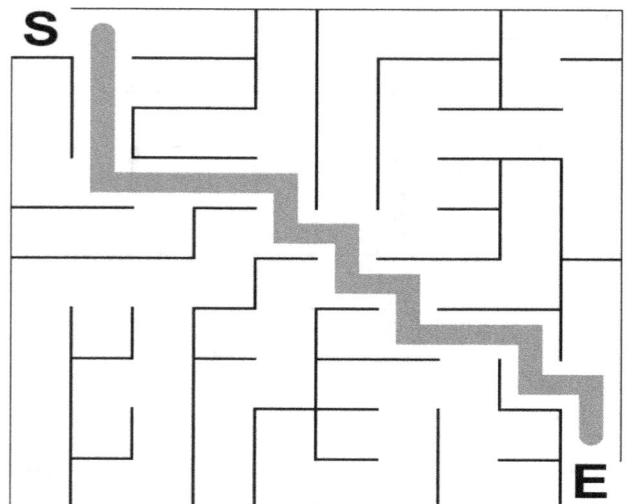

Solution for Puzzle 8

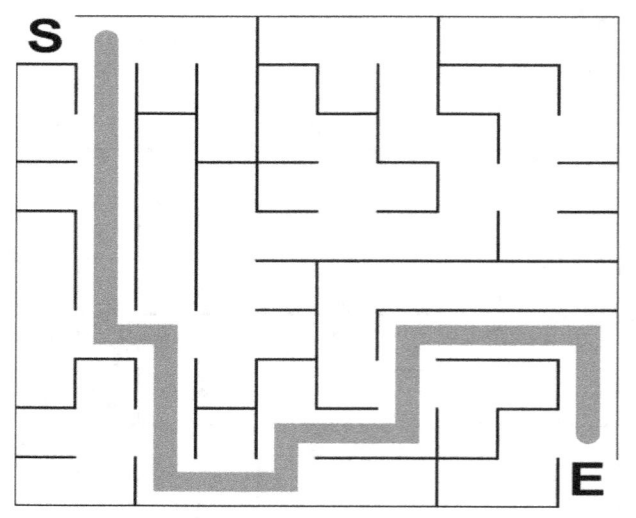

MAZE PUZZLE SOLUTION

75

Solution for Puzzle 9

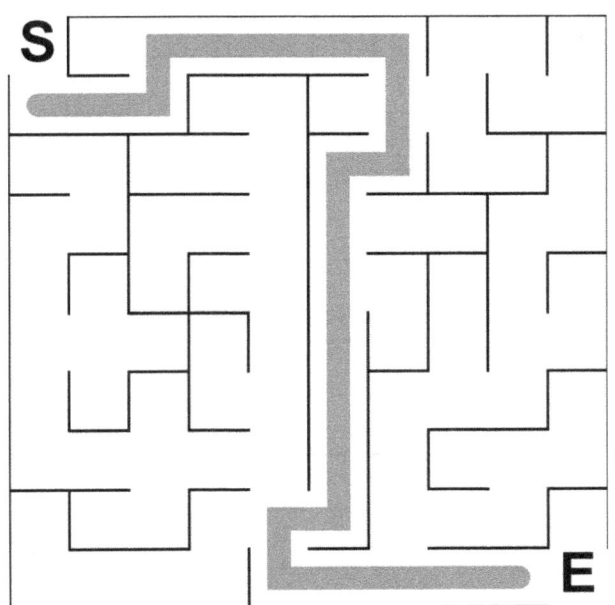

Solution for Puzzle 10

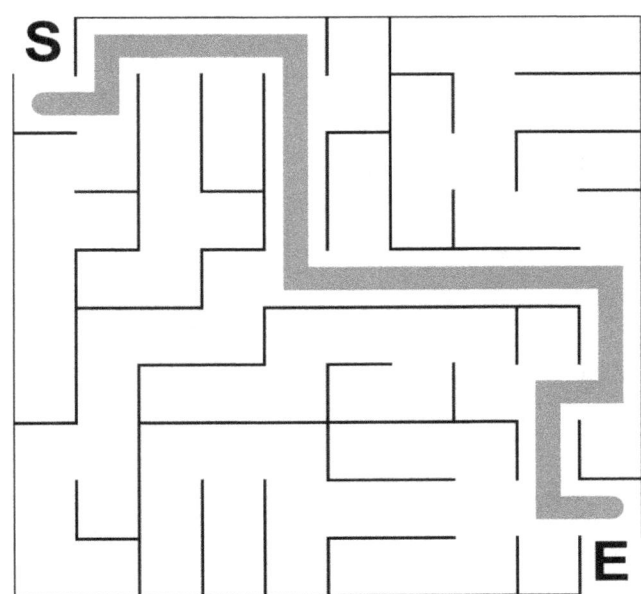

Solution for Puzzle 11

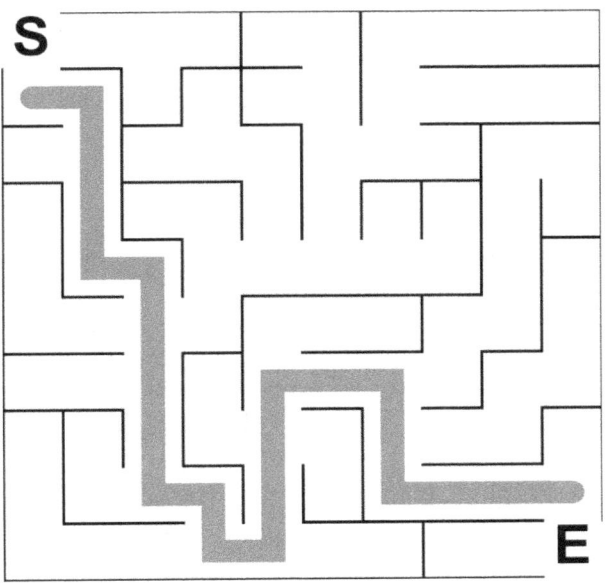

Solution for Puzzle 12

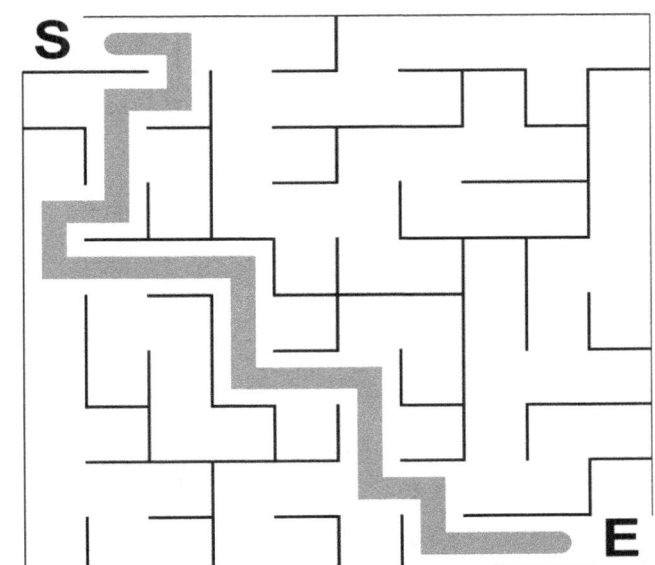

MAZE PUZZLE SOLUTION

76

Solution for Puzzle 13

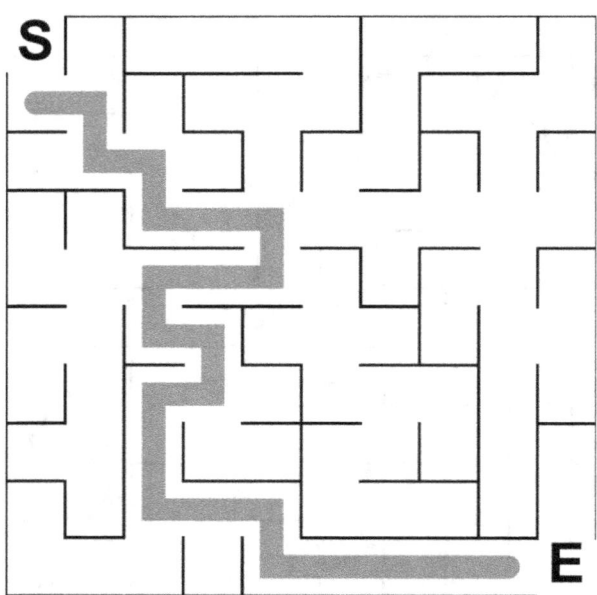

Solution for Puzzle 14

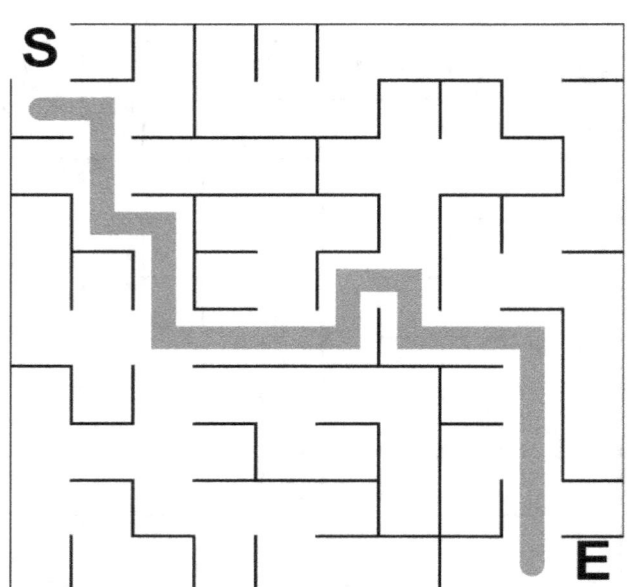

Solution for Puzzle 15

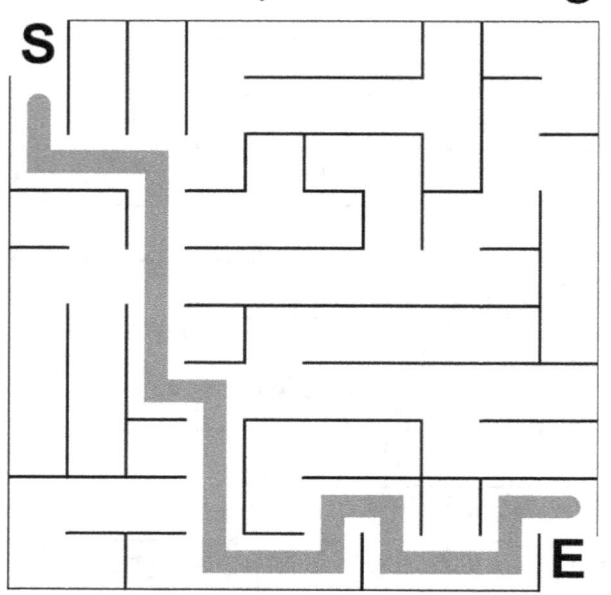

Solution for Puzzle 16

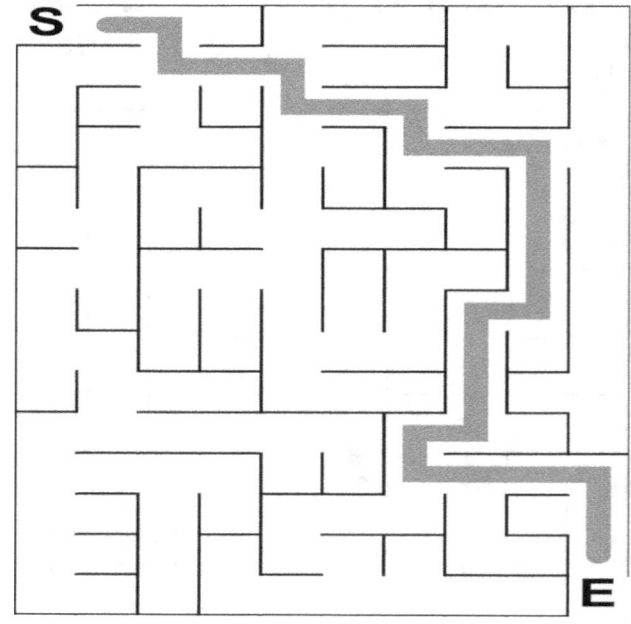

MAZE PUZZLE SOLUTION

Solution for Puzzle 17

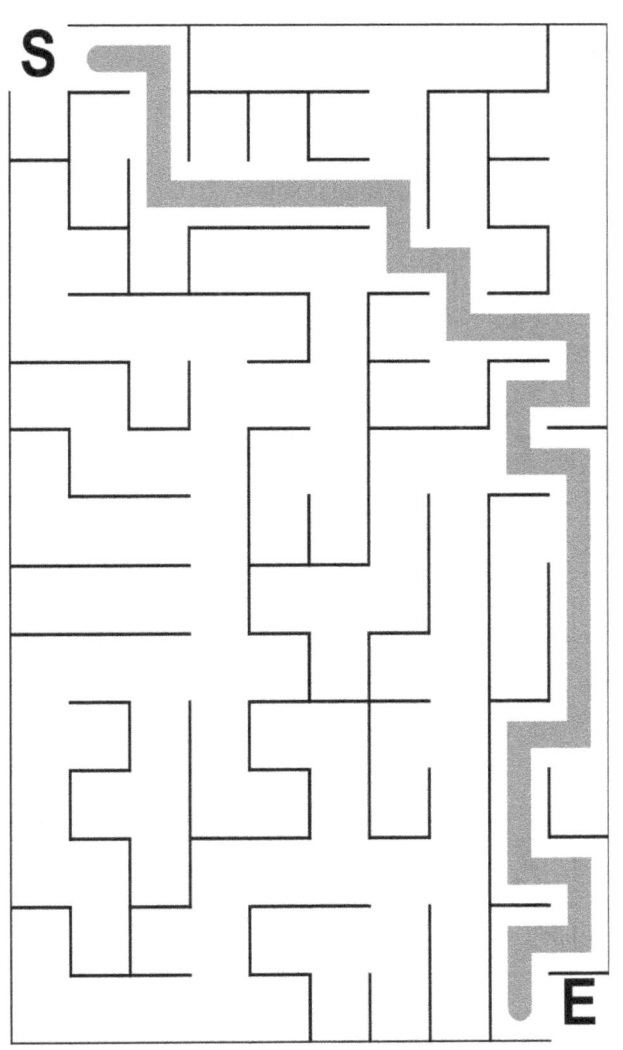

Solution for Puzzle 18

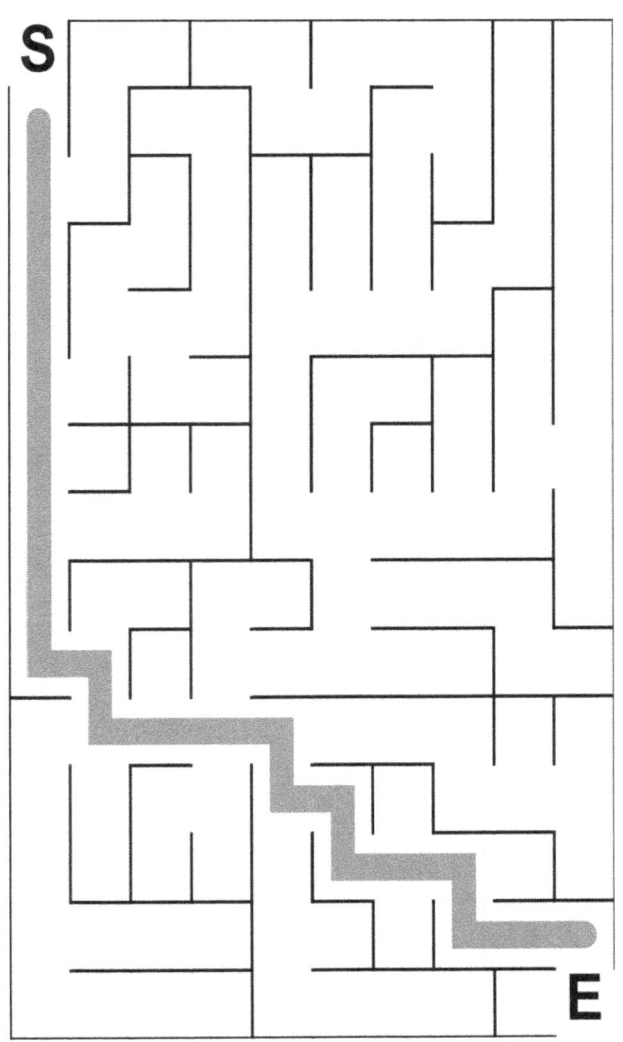

MAZE PUZZLE SOLUTION

Solution for Puzzle 19   Solution for Puzzle 20

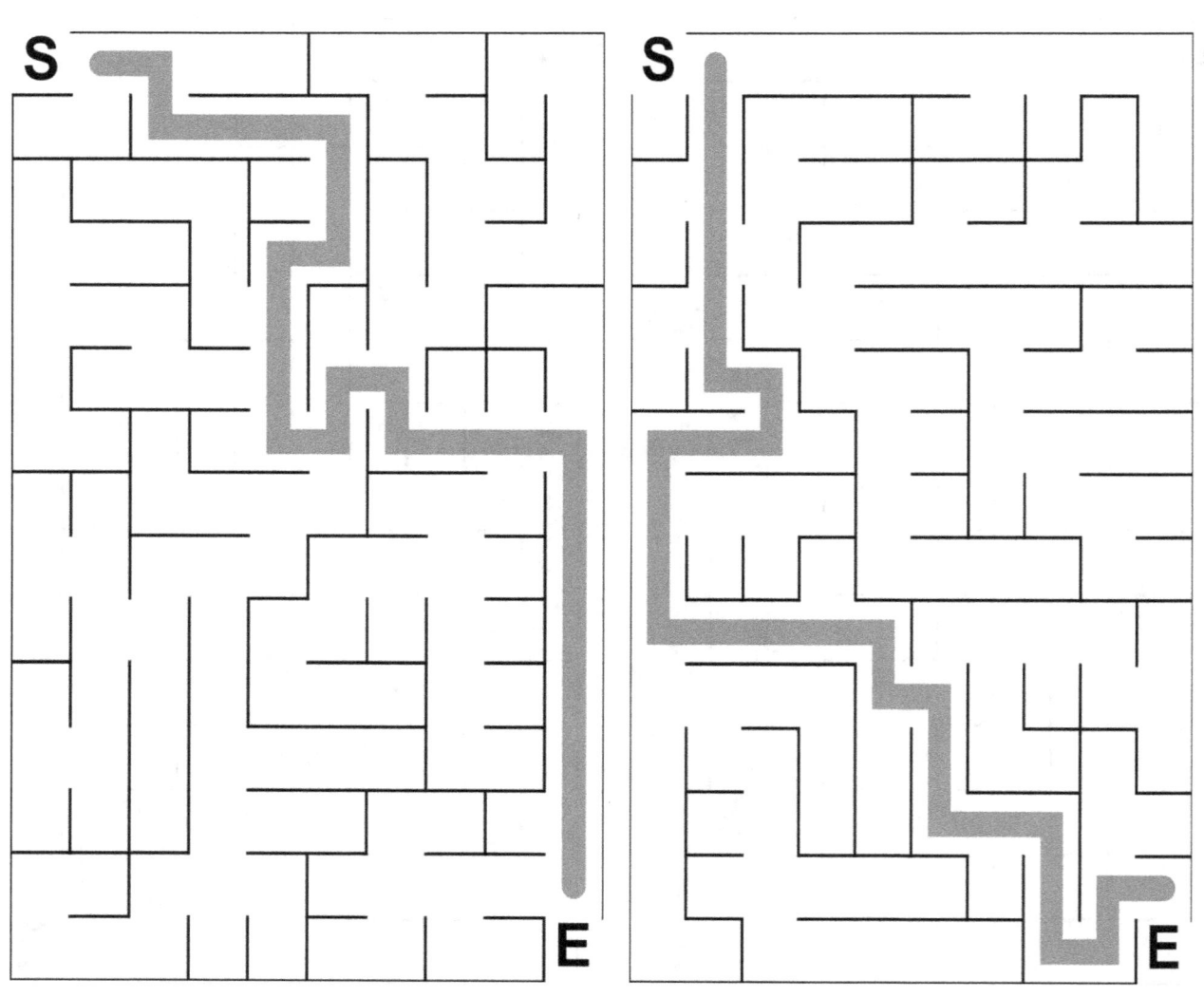

MAZE PUZZLE SOLUTION

Solution for Puzzle 21

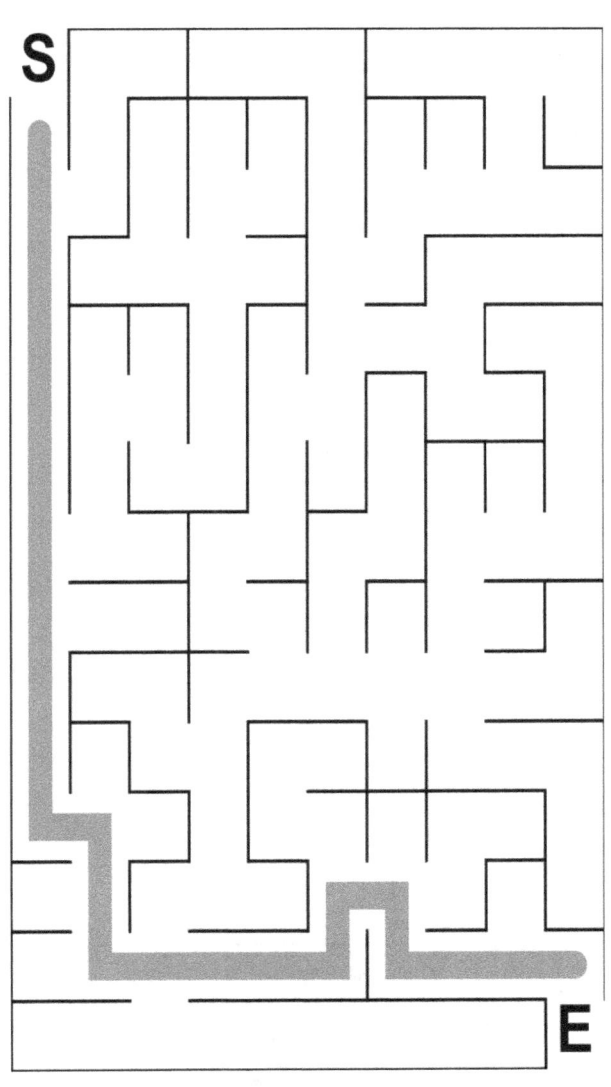

Solution for Puzzle 22

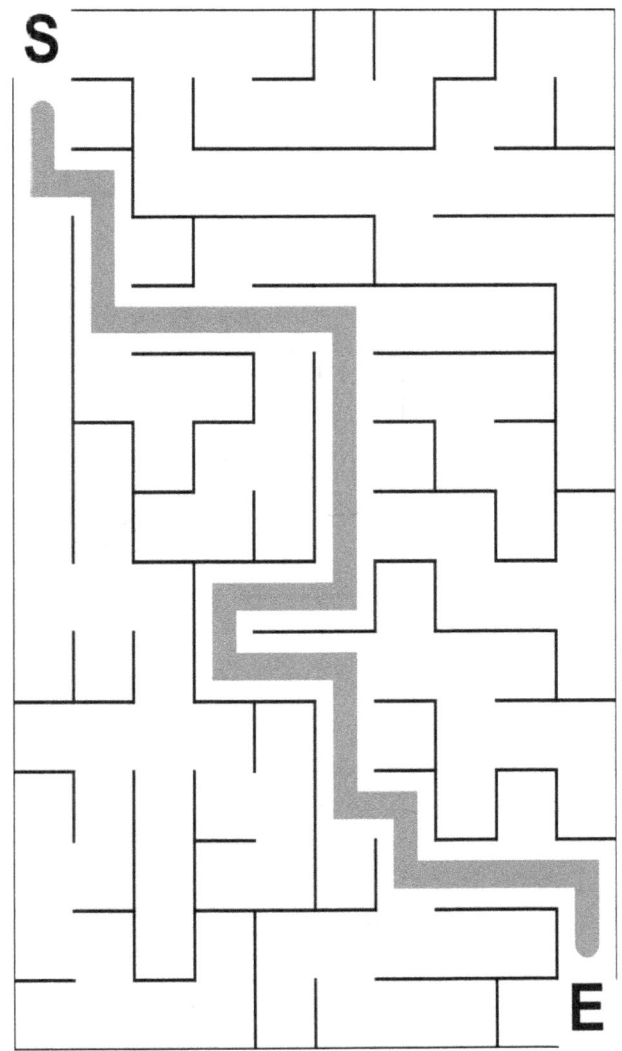

MAZE PUZZLE SOLUTION

Solution for Puzzle 23

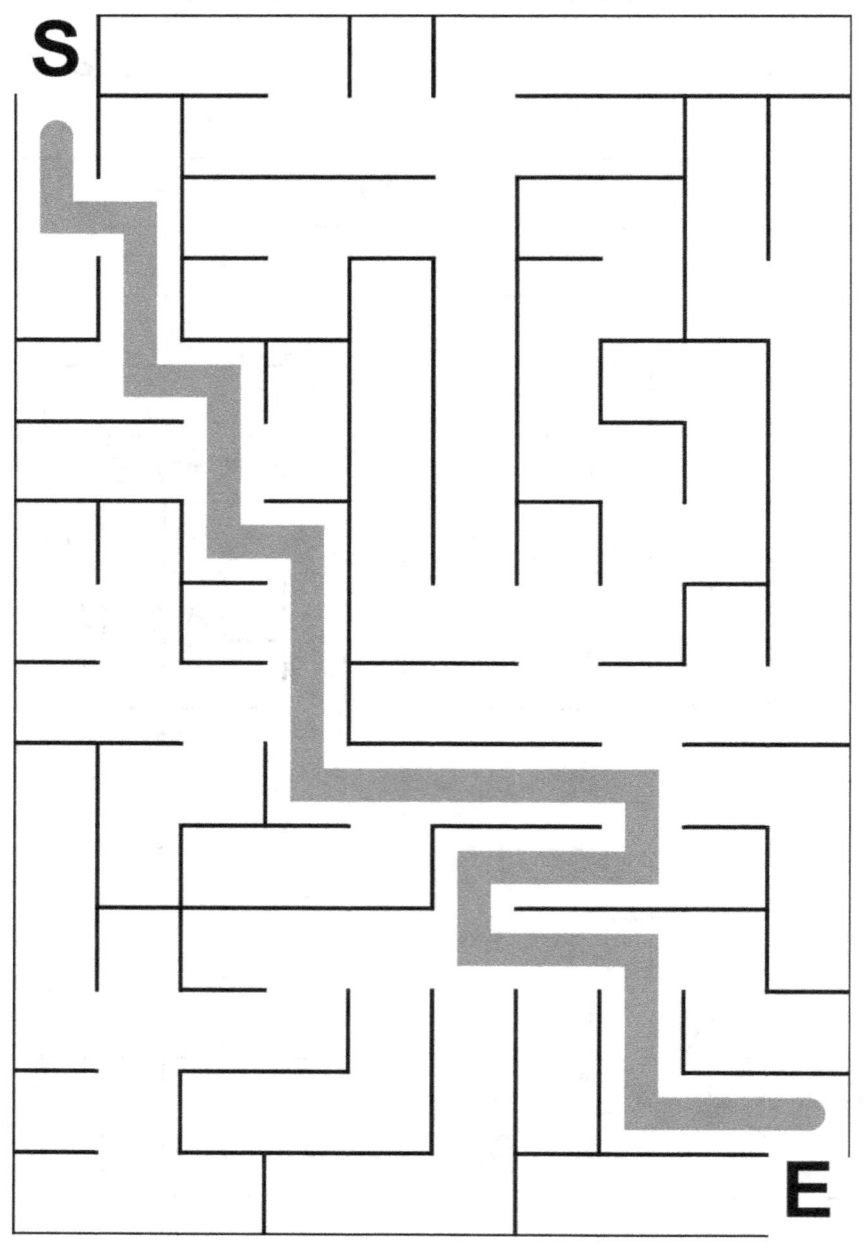

SUDOKU PUZZLE SOLUTION

Solution for Puzzle 43

4	1	2	3
3	2	1	4
1	4	3	2
2	3	4	1

Solution for Puzzle 44

1	2	4	3
4	3	1	2
2	1	3	4
3	4	2	1

SUDOKU PUZZLE SOLUTION

Solution for Puzzle 45

2	1	4	3
3	4	1	2
1	2	3	4
4	3	2	1

Solution for Puzzle 46

4	3	1	2
1	2	4	3
3	4	2	1
2	1	3	4

SUDOKU PUZZLE SOLUTION

Solution for Puzzle 47

1	3	2	4
4	2	3	1
2	4	1	3
3	1	4	2

Solution for Puzzle 48

2	3	4	1
1	4	3	2
3	2	1	4
4	1	2	3

SUDOKU PUZZLE SOLUTION

Solution for Puzzle 49

4	1	3	2
3	2	4	1
2	3	1	4
1	4	2	3

Solution for Puzzle 50

3	4	2	1
2	1	3	4
1	2	4	3
4	3	1	2

SUDOKU PUZZLE SOLUTION

Solution for Puzzle 51

2	3	1	4
1	4	2	3
4	1	3	2
3	2	4	1

Solution for Puzzle 52

4	3	1	2
1	2	4	3
3	4	2	1
2	1	3	4

SUDOKU PUZZLE SOLUTION

Solution for Puzzle 53

3	2	4	1
4	1	3	2
1	4	2	3
2	3	1	4

Solution for Puzzle 54

4	3	1	2
1	2	4	3
3	4	2	1
2	1	3	4

SUDOKU PUZZLE SOLUTION

Solution for Puzzle 55

1	4	3	2
2	3	4	1
3	2	1	4
4	1	2	3

Solution for Puzzle 56

3	4	2	1
1	2	4	3
2	1	3	4
4	3	1	2

SUDOKU PUZZLE SOLUTION

Solution for Puzzle 57

1	2	4	3
4	3	1	2
3	4	2	1
2	1	3	4

Solution for Puzzle 58

3	2	1	4
4	1	2	3
1	4	3	2
2	3	4	1

SUDOKU PUZZLE SOLUTION

Solution for Puzzle 59

3	2	4	1
4	1	3	2
1	4	2	3
2	3	1	4

Solution for Puzzle 60

4	1	3	2
3	2	4	1
2	3	1	4
1	4	2	3

SUDOKU PUZZLE SOLUTION

90

Solution for Puzzle 61

3	2	1	4
4	1	2	3
2	3	4	1
1	4	3	2

Solution for Puzzle 62

3	2	1	4
4	1	2	3
1	4	3	2
2	3	4	1

CAT SHAPED WORD SEARCH SOLUTION

91

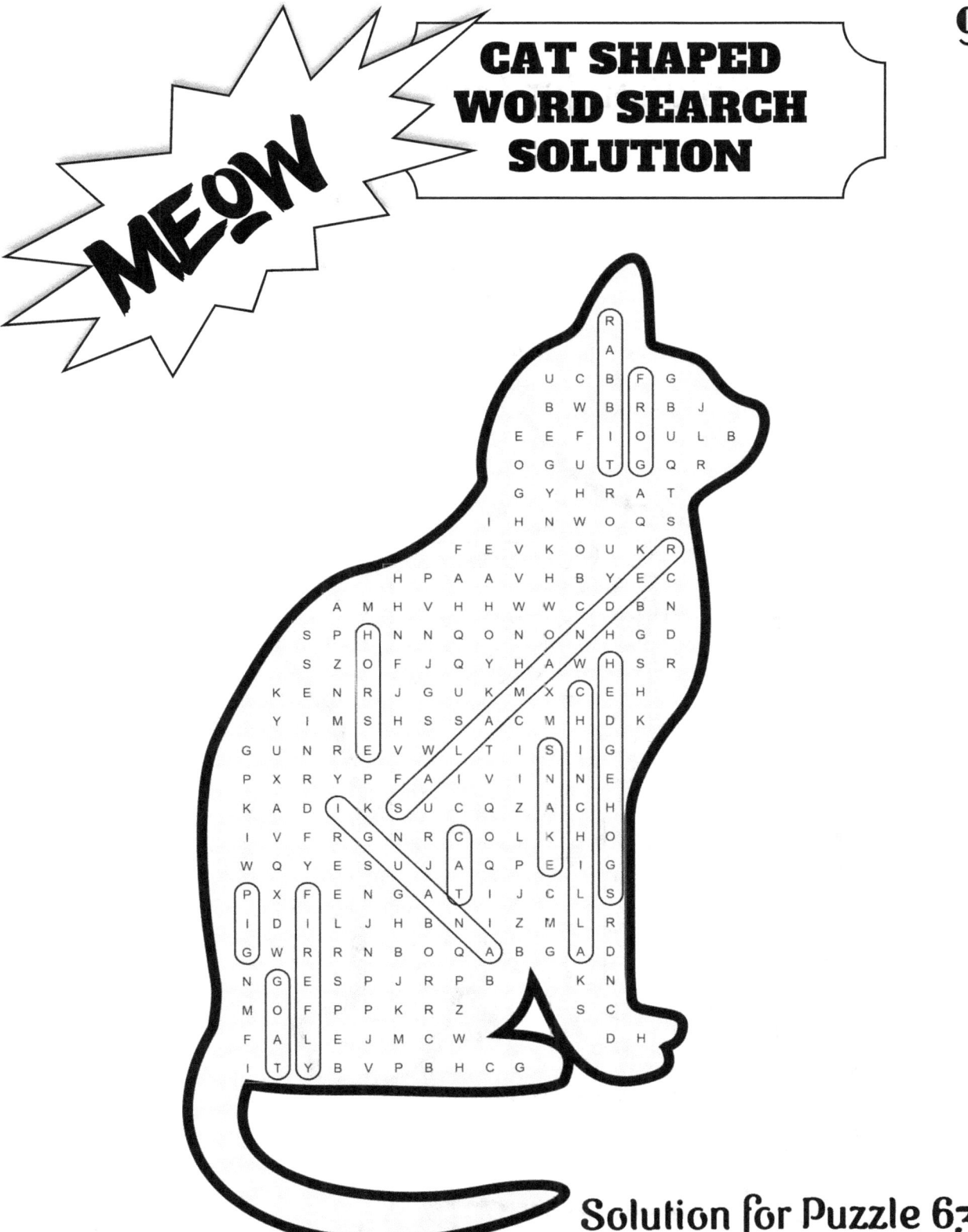

Solution for Puzzle 63

Solution for Puzzle 64

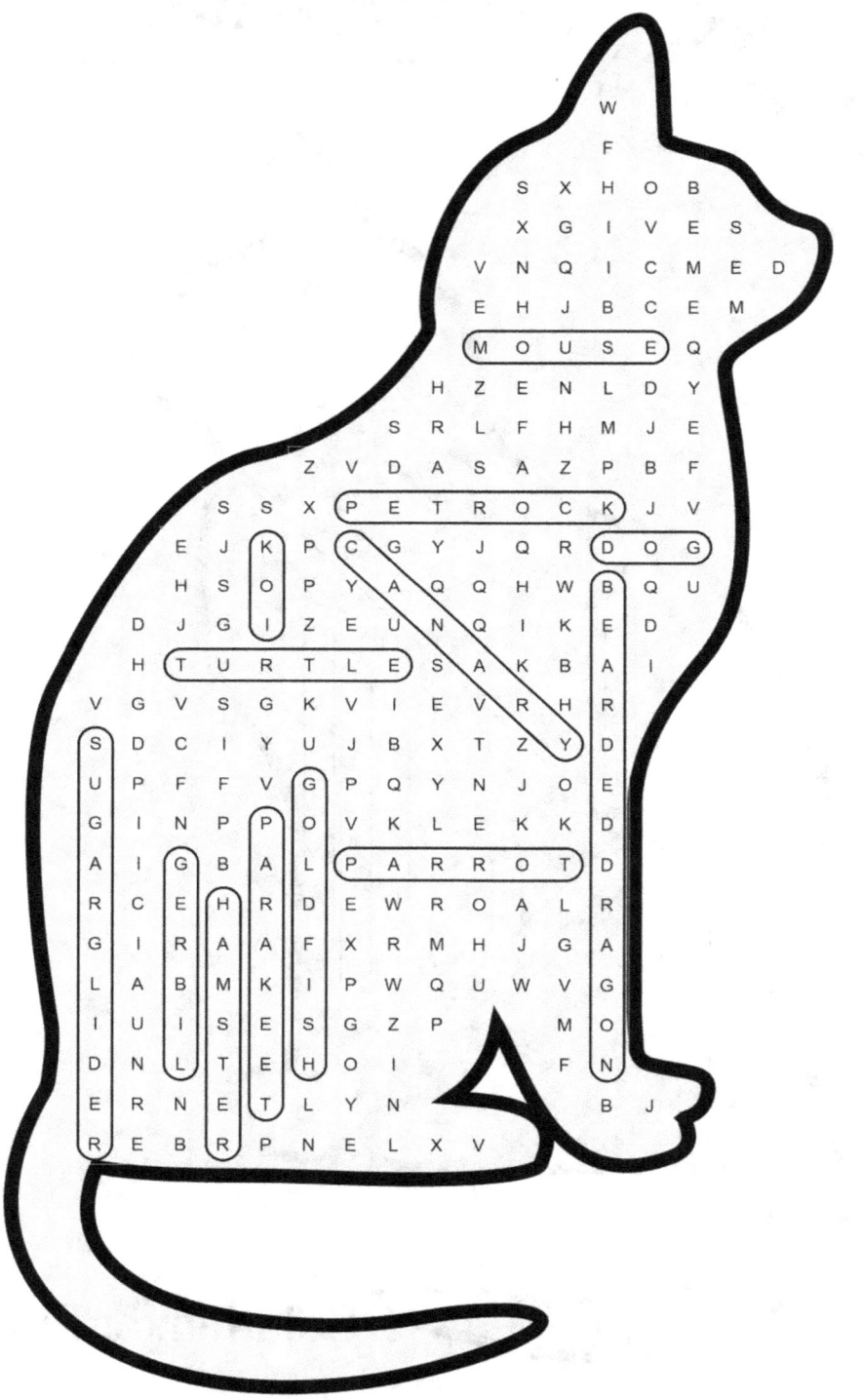

Solution for Puzzle 65

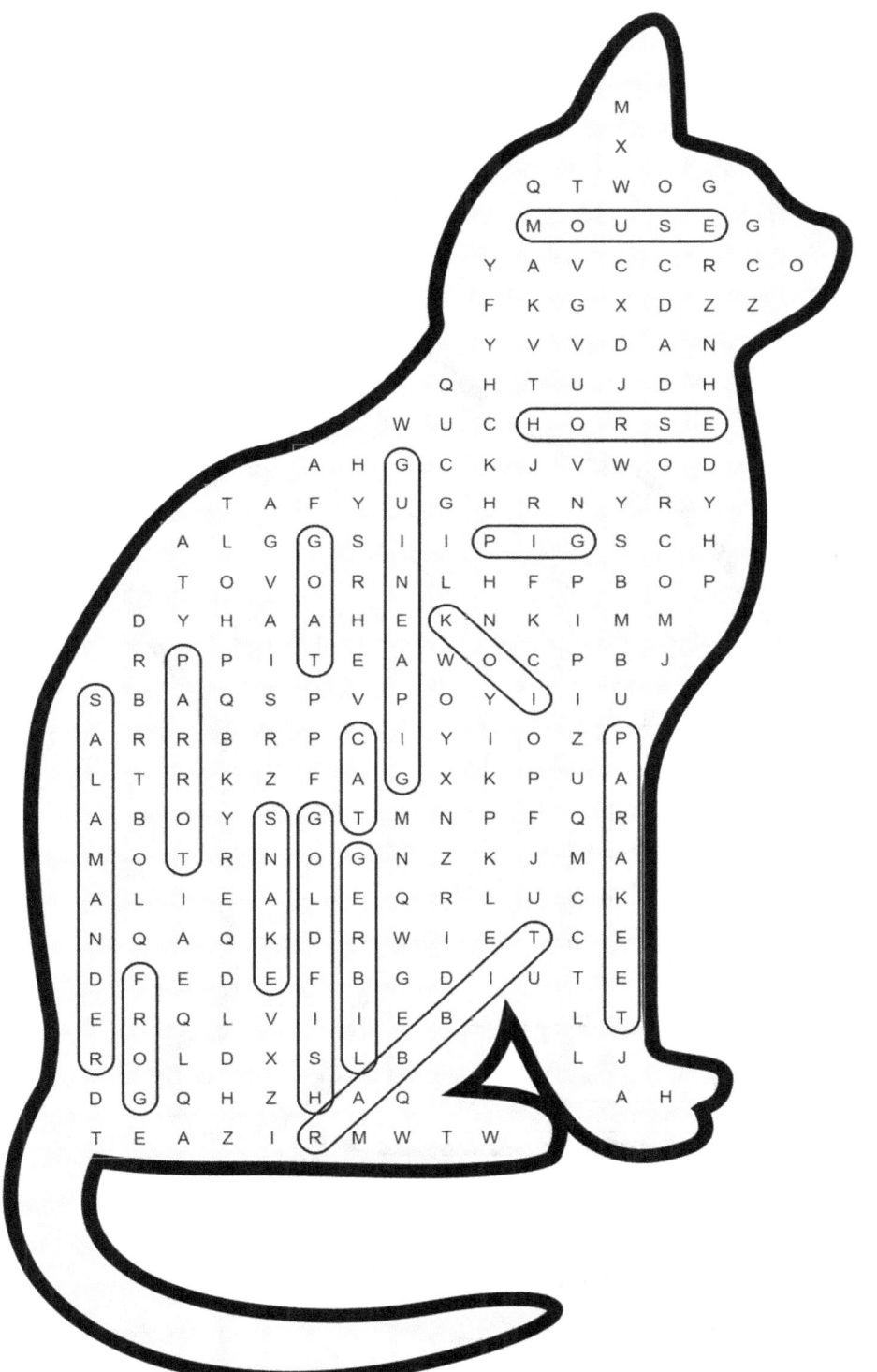

Solution for Puzzle 66

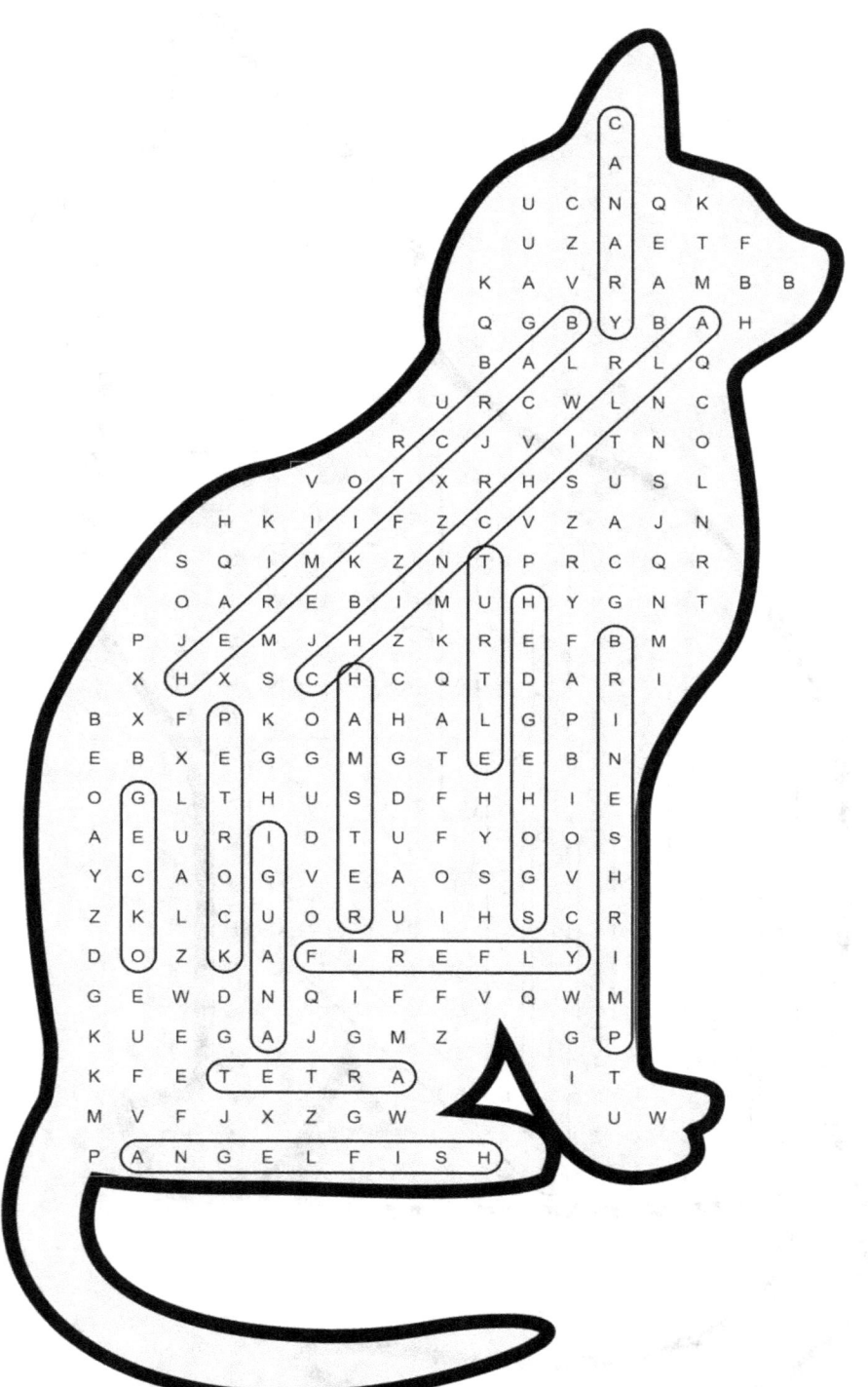

Solution for Puzzle 67

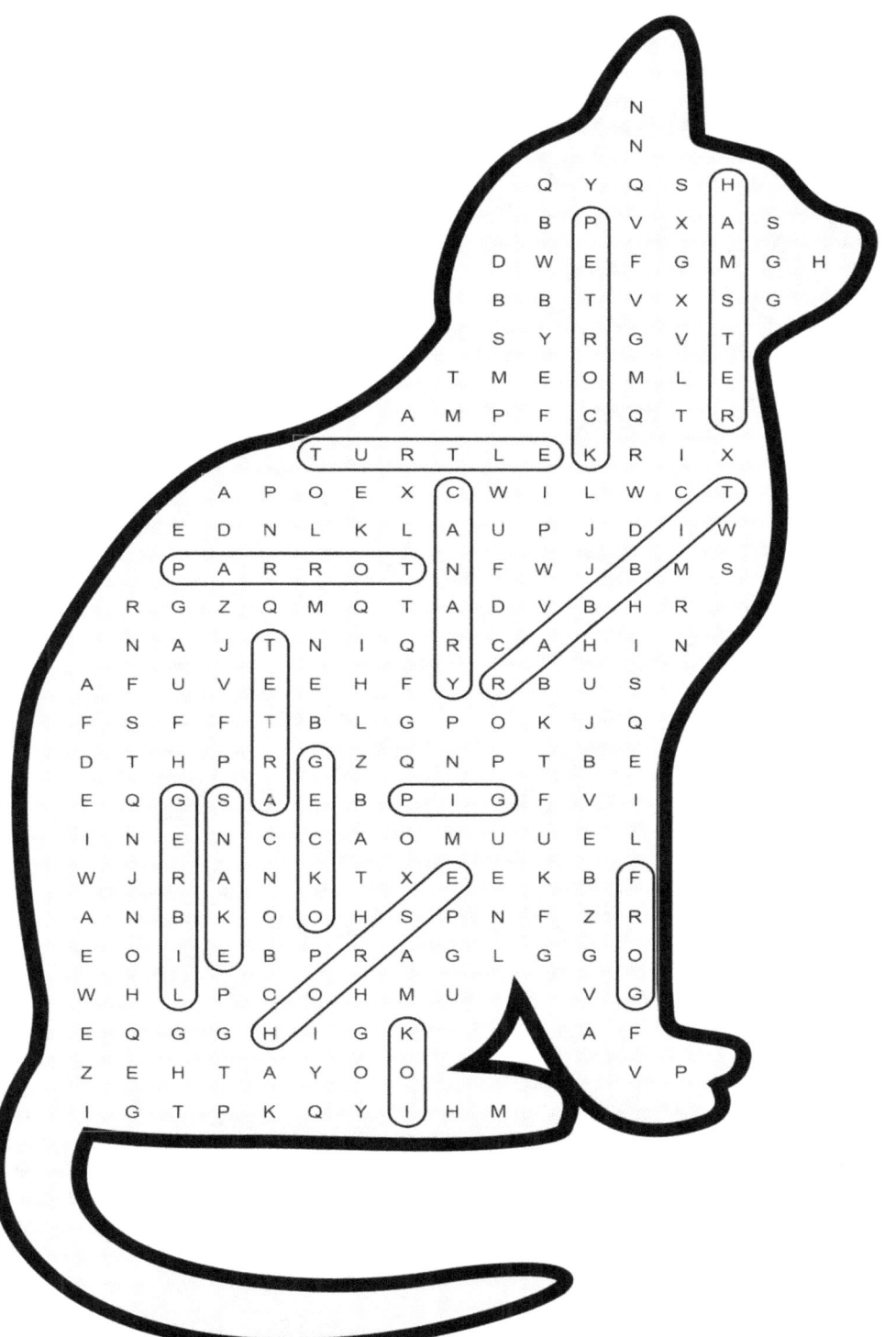

www.ingramcontent.com/pod-product-compliance
Lightning Source LLC
Chambersburg PA
CBHW080609220526
45466CB00010B/3299